I0816212

FENWAY PUNK

FENWAY PUNK

HOW A BOSTON INDIE LABEL SCORED BIG ON BASEBALL'S GREATEST RIVALRY

CHRIS WRENN

RUNNING PRESS
PHILADELPHIA

Note from author:
This work depicts actual events in my life as truthfully as my recollection permits and/ or can be verified by research. Occasionally, dialogue consistent with the character or nature of the person speaking has been supplemented or re-created. All persons within are actual individuals; there are no composite characters. The names of some individuals have been changed to respect their privacy.

Running Press
Hachette Book Group
1290 Avenue of the Americas, New York, NY 10104
www.runningpress.com
@Running_Press

First Edition: February 2026

Published by Running Press, an imprint of Hachette Book Group, Inc. The Running Press name and logo are trademarks of Hachette Book Group, Inc.

The Hachette Speakers Bureau provides a wide range of authors for speaking events. To find out more, go to www.hachettespeakersbureau.com or email HachetteSpeakers@hbgusa.com.

Running Press books may be purchased in bulk for business, educational, or promotional use. For more information, please contact your local bookseller or the Hachette Book Group Special Markets Department at Special.Markets@hbgusa.com.

The publisher is not responsible for websites (or their content) that are not owned by the publisher.

Print book cover and interior design by Joshua G. Lunsk and Susan Van Horn
Photo insert design by Chris Wrenn

Image credits: Front cover photo featuring Wes Eisold courtesy of Bryan Sheffield.
Back cover photo featuring street vendors courtesy of Kate Bowen.
All interior photography courtesy of the author.

Song lyric credits: "Scratch the Surface" (Sick of It All) courtesy of Sick of It All; "Straight Edge" (Minor Threat) courtesy of Dischord Records; "First and Ten" (Ten Yard Fight) courtesy of Ten Yard Fight; "Hearts" (American Nightmare) courtesy of Wes Eisold; "Hard Bark on the Family Tree (Have Heart) courtesy of Patrick Flynn.

Library of Congress Cataloging-in-Publication Data has been applied for.

ISBNs: 979-8-89414-087-2 (hardcover), 979-8-89414-089-6 (ebook)

Printed in the United States of America

LSC-C

Printing 1, 2025

In memory of
Al Barile (SS Decontrol)
and
Jimmy Flynn (Hardcore Stadium)

CONTENTS

PROLOGUE 1

CHAPTER 1:
The Curse of the Bambino 7

CHAPTER 2:
Scratch the Surface 13

CHAPTER 3:
9 Sewall 26

CHAPTER 4:
10.17.99 35

CHAPTER 5:
Y2K 45

CHAPTER 6:
American Nightmare 51

CHAPTER 7:
Disruption 61

CHAPTER 8:
The Sketchy Lot 77

CHAPTER 9:
On the Map 81

CHAPTER 10:
The Bouncer 85

CHAPTER 11:
Us Against Them 91

CHAPTER 12:
Collateral Damage 103

CHAPTER 13:
Initech 109

CHAPTER 14:
Any Band 117

CHAPTER 15:
Nine-Eleven 123

CHAPTER 16:
Hustle 129

CHAPTER 17:
Witch City 147

CHAPTER 18:
The 2003 American League Championship Series 155

CHAPTER 19:
Sully's 161

CHAPTER 20:
Concessions 169

CHAPTER 21:
Competition 175

CHAPTER 22:
Death Before Dishonor 183

CHAPTER 23:
I'm Just Messing with You 187

CHAPTER 24:
Believe in Boston 191

CHAPTER 25:
Redemption 207

CHAPTER 26:
Five Years Later 213

AFTERWORD 221

Acknowledgments 229

PROLOGUE

THURSDAY, MAY 11, 2000. I COULD HEAR A POLICE CAR SIREN from a few streets over; the familiar whine no longer raised an eyebrow as it faded into Boston's Mission Hill neighborhood where I lived. In the 1980s and '90s, the three-quarters-of-a-square-mile area was grittier than it is today; its nickname, "Mission Kill," was well earned back then, primarily due to drug- and gang-related violence. It was most notorious for the 1989 Carol Stuart murder, a crime that gained national attention when Charles Stuart shot his white pregnant wife in their car before shooting himself in the stomach, blaming a fictional, unknown African American assailant who had allegedly tried to rob them. Carol later died at the hospital, which prompted a citywide search for a Black man who didn't exist and led to rising racial tensions. The murder was an attempt to cash in on a life-insurance policy, and Charles eventually jumped from the Tobin Bridge into the dark waters of the Mystic River in an early-morning suicide. While the original account of the assault on the couple had been made up, crime in Mission Hill was a genuine issue and initially lent credibility to his story, as the city saw a high of 152 murders the same year he took his own life. By 1999, murders in Boston had dropped to a reportedly historic low of only 31 after the city made significant efforts to increase neighborhood policing.

It was late that night, and I was in bed beside Elisabeth, whom I'd recently started dating. She was a petite dark-haired woman with more tattoos than I had. We'd been introduced to each other at a punk-rock show by a mutual friend months earlier and had hit it off. Her apartment was five minutes away from mine, and I was staying there more often. My place had a cluttered warehouse feel, with art supplies and brown cardboard boxes stacked to the ceiling on industrial steel shelves—the kind you get at a home improvement store. My bed was the bottom half of a wooden bunk I'd had since I was a kid. The apartment was in a narrow town house overrun by skateboarders, punk-music fans, and empty beer cans. Someone was always up, and something was always happening into the early morning. Conversely, Elisabeth shared a much quieter apartment with two other professional women and had a bathroom with a reliable supply of toilet paper.

My cell phone vibrated from under the covers. I felt around in the dark, trying to find it before it sent the call to voicemail. It was my first mobile phone and I'd carefully placed it on the bed, yet it had been pushed out of reach.

"Hello?" I answered as I sat up in bed.

"Want to make some money?" my friend Matt blurted out.

"Always," I said with a laugh as I listened to him give his best pitch about what our group of friends was up to and why he was calling. After a moment of consideration, I responded. "Are you serious? Yeah, sure, fuck it. I'll head over."

"Who was that?" Elisabeth asked. I swung my legs over the side of her bed and turned the knob on the lamp on her dresser, waiting a moment for my eyes to adjust to the sudden brightness before finding my jeans on the floor. I pulled the dark denim over my legs and explained what I'd just agreed to do.

"That was Galle," I said, referring to Matt by his more frequently used last name. "The guys want to see a fight, and they've got $500 for the winner, so I volunteered."

It was an opportunity conceived from sheer boredom. Friends had pooled enough prize money to convince two of us to punch each other repeatedly for it—winner takes all. The first to accept the challenge was Davey, a new face in the neighborhood. He gave off a younger-brother vibe and was down to do anything, especially when money was involved. I'd later learn that Galle had initially agreed to the fight but had backed out, so he'd been tasked with finding someone to take his place. For that kind of money, I was willing.

Elisabeth sat there in apparent unease as she took in the details. Her furrowed brow told me she was uncomfortable with my leaving under these circumstances.

"Wait, you're going to fight someone for money?" She stared at me in disbelief as I stood up.

"Yeah, but I'll need to win if I want to keep it," I replied, unaware this was being interpreted as a relationship red flag. I smiled as I slipped out the door and said, "Don't worry, I'll be right back."

I descended the wooden front-porch stairs and began my late-night trek across Mission Hill to Galle's apartment. The neighborhood wasn't exceptionally well lit: every block, a lone streetlamp cast its dim light on a small stretch of sidewalk. I startled a skunk inside a knocked-over garbage can, causing it to shuffle toward the darkness between the row houses. A police car drove past me slowly but continued down the road ahead. Music and loud voices emanated from a party inside an apartment nearby; a party was always happening somewhere on Mission Hill.

As I walked to Galle's place, I began to second-guess myself. I wasn't exactly the "get in the ring" type like a few of the guys I hung out with. Most of the fights I'd been in had been spontaneous—the kind you didn't have time to think about beforehand—and were usually over as quickly as they started. My friend Rod, though, who was likely the mastermind behind this prizefight, was known to pull his shirt off over his head at the slightest provocation, ready to start swinging. That wasn't my vibe, and the last time I'd met up with someone to square off was a middle-school fistfight in a neighbor's backyard a decade earlier. What if this didn't go my way? I wouldn't be able to live it down.

Despite my concern, my gut said this wouldn't be a fair fight for Davey. I had a few inches on him, but I also figured I needed the money more than he did. And unless he secretly knew jujitsu or some other martial art, I knew I'd walk home $500 richer.

I jogged up the stairs and entered the second floor of Galle's Cherokee Street apartment, where there was a flurry of activity. It was late, but not for these guys, and the excitement was palpable. I was greeted with a few high-fives in the narrow hallway. "Let's all go to the Sketchy Lot," shouted Tony Pops, referring to the old parking lot down the street.

"A cop passed me on my way over; we might want to keep this indoors, maybe head to the basement," I said.

"Naw, this shit's going out to the Sketchy Lot, dude," replied Derek Wentz, a Southern California transplant who someone had nicknamed Rusty because he looked like the youngest Griswold in the movie *National Lampoon's Vacation*. He carried a video camera; they wouldn't miss the chance to document this. We walked in a single file down the stairwell, spilled out into the night, turned the corner onto Pontiac Street, and scoped out the scene.

"Shouldn't they fight on grass?" asked Galle.

"At least dirt," responded Rusty, laughing.

As we approached the lot, our friend Worm pointed at a corner of it and exclaimed, "Right there is the fight zone."

Friends first called him Perm because he'd once sported curly hair. Then someone started calling him Worm the Perm, and soon after, it became just Worm. Worm was a hustler with a reputation for doing anything for money, like scalping bootleg concert tickets at music festivals and selling counterfeit VHS tapes of new movies off folding tables on the sidewalk. None of us had jobs that paid well, so we all needed side hustles, but for Worm, the side hustles *were* his job.

We settled on a section of the lot with a partially obstructed view from the road thanks to a shoulder-high stone wall. Yells of excitement led to pleas for quiet after Worm shoved Davey toward me as a van slowly drove by. We didn't want to blow up our spot before things got started.

I could see the Sketchy Lot from the steps of my first apartment in Boston and had walked past it hundreds of times in the two years I had lived in the neighborhood. It stretched about a half-block down the street and had earned its nickname because it looked like it was from an episode of *Life After People*, the TV series that chronicled how things would deteriorate in the decades after people vanished from Earth. The crumbling asphalt had long blades of grass and weeds growing through the cracks. A steep granite wall bordered the lot, unevenly spray-painted with layers of graffiti tags along the rocky edge. It was a terrible spot to park a car—likely why it was usually empty—but as far as places to fight someone at one in the morning went, it looked pretty good. Everyone stood around us in anticipation, hoping we'd give them a good show.

Davey and I squared up in the middle of a roughly horseshoe-shaped outline of our friends. He'd removed his shirt and was swinging his arms inward as he loosened up. The Mission Hill Basilica's twin church spires were darkly silhouetted before Boston's nighttime skyline. They towered just behind us, more than two hundred feet in the air, a crucifix glowing brightly on each, and on the horizon behind them in the distance, the light on the top of the Prudential Center building blinked.

"Is kicking allowed?" Galle asked.

"No rules," Worm replied.

"Who's got the video camera?" Jamey chimed in.

"I do, dickhead!" responded Rusty.

I smiled at Davey and casually asked, "What's going on, dude?" as we slowly began circling each other in front of the rock wall at the edge of the lot.

"C'mon, guys, yeah!" shouted Rusty as he pointed the camera toward us. "Let's do this shit!"

I raised my fists up in front of my face as our crew of friends shouted our names, offering us both words of encouragement. I tried to focus on my opponent, but I was also imagining the stack of cash I would be shoving into my pocket should I end up beating his ass. I was always down to make a buck. At thirteen years of age I had placed flyers for "Chris's Helping Hands" in my neighbors' mailboxes, offering to cut lawns and clean out garages. That drive to earn money grew stronger, and now in my early twenties, I was making sure to still use my hands to grab every dollar I could.

CHAPTER 1

The Curse of the Bambino

IF YOU WALKED BY FENWAY PARK, THE HISTORIC HOME FIELD of the Boston Red Sox baseball team, on a summer evening in 1999 when a game was happening, you'd hear tens of thousands of people chanting in unison, "Yankees suck! Yankees suck!"

It was the most heard phrase in Boston that summer, and whenever fans started chanting it from the bleachers, everyone inside Fenway Park joined in. The New York Yankees, longtime rivals of the Red Sox, had won two of the last three World Series championships, and people in Boston despised both the team and their fans. The chant was a unifying mantra that brought every Sox fan together, if only for a few choruses. It let them express their mutual disdain for the team that had bested the Red Sox for so many years. By the time I heard it, generations of fans had chanted it. It always started as a handful of people and built up to an overwhelming roar as thousands joined in.

The reality, though, was that the Yankees didn't suck. Not even a little bit. Over the past century they'd won baseball's top trophy a league-leading twenty-four times, while the Red Sox had earned just five. Starting with the first World Series in 1903, Boston's early-twentieth-century winning streak was short-lived, leading to one of the most prolonged championship droughts in professional sports. The most recent Red Sox victory had been in 1918, during the final months of the First World War and a year before the team's cash-strapped owner sold future Hall of Famer George Herman "Babe" Ruth—a.k.a. the Bambino—to the Yankees. It was a transaction that distressed Boston fans at the time because Babe Ruth, as he was known, was the superstar of his day. The winning abruptly ceased, and the Red Sox were said to have fallen under the Curse of the Bambino, a superstition that was blamed for every mishap in the eight decades since the Red Sox last won a World Series.

Before the Babe Ruth trade, the Yankees had yet to even make it to the World Series, much less win. In the years after, they dominated the league. Cemeteries in Massachusetts filled with fans who went to their graves never having seen the Red Sox go all the way. The team perfected the art of losing dramatically when it counted the most. Years of watching the Yankees advance to the World Series and win it all created a deep-seated resentment from Boston fans who didn't like the rival team, their deep-pocketed owners, or the smugness of their fans. Chanting "Yankees suck" with thousands of others was a cathartic way of saying fuck you to all of them.

The chant was inescapable when the Yankees were in town, but it broke out at some point during every game in Boston, whether New York was even playing or not. When another team visited with fans who also hated the Yankees, it was twice as loud. That was the thing: hating the Yankees wasn't exclusive to Sox fans—it was especially vigorous in Boston, because the two teams duked it out regularly in the American League (AL) division, playing each other sixteen or more times per season, but the sentiment extended nationwide. And it wasn't limited to games; you would also hear "Yankees suck" chants at concerts, outdoor events, and even wedding receptions around Massachusetts. In most cities, fans simply rooted for their hometown team. In Boston, hating the Yankees was just as much a part of a fan's identity as supporting the Red Sox.

With few exceptions over the years, Boston hadn't been very competitive, while the Yankees making it to the World Series was essentially guaranteed. During a handful of seasons, the Sox looked promising, but then, by the last stretch of regular-season games in September, they'd shit the bed. The year 1978 should have been their time: the Red Sox peaked that summer with fourteen and a half wins ahead of the Yankees. Instead, the lead was whittled away during the season's final months, ending with what went on to be known as the four-game Boston Massacre series. The Yankees won them all, sweeping the Red Sox, forcing a tie in the American League East division. Both teams had finished the season with ninety-nine wins and sixty-three losses, so Fenway Park hosted a chance to break the tie. Heartbreak came in the form of a three-run homer from Yankees shortstop Bucky Dent, who, at the top of the seventh inning, sent the ball over the fabled left-field scoreboard wall known as the Green Monster, taking a two-run Red Sox advantage and giving New York a 3–2 lead. The Yankees went on to win the World Series again. An entire generation of Red Sox fans still curse Bucky Dent's name.

The Red Sox wouldn't make it to the World Series again until 1986, and as a young fan I hung on to every win, a Sox hat perched backward on my head at all times that season. The Angels almost eliminated the Sox in the best-of-seven American League Championship Series (ALCS) that year, but Boston returned from a 3–1 deficit to advance after winning Game Seven. They kept their streak going by taking the first two World Series games from the New York Mets down in Queens, New York, which improved Boston's odds of winning it all, as they returned home for the next three games. The Mets won Games Four and Five to even the series, but the 1986 Red Sox team would go on to be remembered most for the ground ball that went through first baseman Bill Buckner's legs in Game Six. It should have been an easy out and a win closer to a long-awaited World Series victory for the Red Sox. Instead, it let the Mets continue to fight it out for an extra-innings triumph, allowing them the chance to win it all the following day, collectively breaking the hearts and wills of Red Sox fans everywhere. And that was it—their last trip to the World Series. The Red Sox had mainly unremarkable seasons throughout the 1990s, while the Yankees continued to come out on top, rubbing salt in the wounds of Boston fans almost annually.

"Yankees suck" chants may be synonymous with Boston, but New Yorkers were the ones that started the first "sucks" chants from the grandstands in 1977 when fans insulted the Red Sox by yelling "Boston sucks" as the Sox competed with the Yankees in a particularly contentious pennant race. T-shirts with that phrase followed during the 1978 season, created by an entrepreneurial Yankees fan named Joe Schatzle Jr. Joe first started peddling "I Love NY" tees along Fifth Avenue to tourists in New York City, and his instantly popular "Boston Sucks" T-shirts inspired more chants at Yankee Stadium and even raunchier apparel. In an October 1978 *Boston Globe* article titled "Sox, Yankee Fans Taking Turn for Worse," celebrated sportswriter Peter Gammons described Yankee Stadium by saying, "You can purchase any kind of 'Sucks' t-shirt you want. There are shirts describing what things Red Sox players can do to each other. Shirts that find ten different ways to make Carlton Fisk refuse to allow his wife and kids [to] travel south of Bridgeport." Gammons questioned if the vulgarity had been inspired by "Punk-Chic." In another *Globe* article only weeks earlier, Gammons noted, "What Brooks Brothers button-downs are to [famed Harvard University society] the Porcellian Club, 'Boston Sucks' tee-shirts are to Yankee Stadium."

Boston fans fed the rivalry with "Damn Yankees," "Certified Yankee Hater," and "New York Bites" shirts being sold on the streets around Fenway Park. The latter two gained national attention from a cover story in the premiere issue of *Newsweek*-backed *Inside Sports* magazine in 1979. The shirts had been sold for several seasons off a rack on the street by a pair of enterprising women—best friends Irene Dondley and Debbie Brooks—to people headed into the game. These two women helped establish the market in Boston for rivalry-inspired apparel, allowing fans to express their true feelings in ways that weren't possible from the official team souvenir stores.

The hawking of products around Fenway Park was, and continues to be, a time-honored tradition for street-level entrepreneurs and people willing to hustle. There are a lot of opportunities when thirty-eight thousand people gather in one place eighty-one times a year. Hours before game time, vendors began lining up in the streets and sidewalks around the stadium—peanuts and sausages from carts, souvenirs and sunglasses off folding tables. During the Boston Massacre series in '78, Joe Schatzle Jr. decided to play both sides of the rivalry. He printed twelve hundred of the first "Yankees Suck" tees before driving north to Fenway with three friends to help sell them. An instant hit, the shirts sold out before the fourth and final game. Despite their widespread availability, the shirts had long since worn out of circulation before I arrived on the scene twenty years later.

In 1978, increased publicity surrounding the negative T-shirts led to a crackdown and sudden change in how the stadium coexisted with the culture of independent vendors who sold products to the crowds walking into games. The team brought a barely enforced city ordinance to the attention of the Boston police just before the home stand with the Yankees that September—one stipulating that street vendors needed to move after every sale instead of setting up shop in one location on the sidewalk. As police cleared the streets of independent sellers, officers arrested a third-generation peanut vendor whose grandfather was reportedly the first to hawk peanuts from a cart during Fenway's inaugural 1912 season. It was seen as a cash grab by the new Red Sox ownership to limit the street-level competition with their souvenir shops. They had purchased the team a year earlier for more than $20 million, the most ever spent on a sports franchise, and they wouldn't leave any money on the table or within reach of anyone else.

By the end of the 1990s, the hatred for the Yankees was again boiling over, and Sox fans needed help expressing their feelings when they couldn't shout them aloud. Anyone who offered something taking the piss out of the Yankees again to Red Sox fans stood to make a lot of money.

CHAPTER 2

Scratch the Surface

I WAS AN ANGSTY KID WITH AN ATTENTION DEFICIT HYPERACTIVITY disorder (ADHD) diagnosis. I channeled my energy into skateboarding and spent time with a few like-minded friends. I drank my first beers around the age of thirteen at parties thrown by older neighbors, then tried harder alcohol smuggled by friends into the woods behind our high school after class. It was typical teen-rebellion shit. Later I'd spend weekend nights with the handful of other subculture-seeking allies around campfires, taking hits of shitty weed from a pipe that someone had fashioned from an empty aluminum soda can—all while bonding over a mutual appreciation of heavy metal, punk rock, and skateboarding.

Deep Purple's protometal album *Machine Head* was the first record I owned on vinyl; my cousin Bruce gave me his backup copy when I was ten. It was 1986; I lived in a Connecticut suburb, and until then, I'd listened only to pop radio. That record was my first chance to choose what I heard, and despite the grooves having been worn down before it was passed to me, I spun it repeatedly while memorizing the lyrics to songs like "Highway Star" and "Smoke on the Water." Later, thanks to a gift certificate I'd earned after an orthodontist visit, I purchased a copy of Mötley Crüe's *Girls, Girls, Girls* from a local record store. That album was my first unfiltered look at a world that moved much faster than the one I knew.

The descent into heavy-metal fandom was quick, and by age twelve, Metallica's *Garage Days Re-Revisited* exposed me to the Misfits' brand of horror punk with their covers of the songs "Last Caress" and "Green Hell." Thrash-metal bands with threatening names like Nuclear Assault, Anthrax, and Suicidal Tendencies followed, their loud music blaring from behind the closed door of my bedroom throughout middle school. After seeing an advertisement for the album *Slowly We Rot* by the death-metal band Obituary, I stole a copy from the Tape World music store in the Prudential Center mall in Boston. I was spending Thanksgiving weekend with my family in the city, and I wasn't about to ask my Irish Catholic parents to shell out twelve dollars for a cassette with an illustration of a dead body lying in a gutter on the cover, so I stuck it under my shirt and then spent the next ten minutes hiding in the Payless shoe store next door after the security tag on it set an alarm off as I exited the store. Many of these albums had shocking, violent imagery and lyrics, which to me was great because, as a suburban teenager, I was tired of the safe, trendy bullshit that everyone I knew was into, and I wanted to be shocked. But it came with a price. People called it "kill your mother music" where I lived and labeled fans as freaks and outcasts.

By 1992, my love of metal music was eclipsed by my growing interest in hardcore punk, and friends and I started carpooling around the state to watch bands as they performed in small clubs, legion halls, and basements. To the uninitiated, hardcore-punk music has the intensity of heavy metal but is raw and stripped down like punk. The bands weren't singing about horror and fantasy, but rather about subjects I could relate to more closely, like questioning authority, being yourself, and finding your place in the world. For less than ten bucks, you could see four or five bands perform in a tiny venue without a barrier between the stage and the people in the audience. These shows could—and still can—get out of control. Aggressive mosh pits formed, and I found myself with my back pressed against a wall, unfamiliar with what was happening. Until this point, the live music I'd witnessed had been from the comfort of a seat, hundreds of feet from the stage. I now had to watch the crowd as much as the band to avoid the unpredictable barrage of fists and feet that inevitably came my way. It wasn't just about what happened onstage; everyone in the room became part of the experience. It was intimidating, but I was hooked.

My favorite band was Sick of It All: New York hardcore stalwarts who had made a name for themselves with their high-energy, chaotic, and often dangerous live performances. They were one of the few hardcore bands being interviewed in magazines that covered heavy metal at the time. The opening song on their first album started with the vocalist shouting, "It's clobberin' time," and I loved it. Their breakout album released in 1994, *Scratch the Surface*, featured the lyrics: "Scratch the surface, serve a purpose / Scratch the surface, don't waste my time." That struck a chord with me. I may have had the slacker-skateboarder schtick down, but I wanted to do something and make a mark. That's likely what attracted me to graffiti. High school friends and I passed around a stolen copy of the spray-paint bible *Subway Art* and practiced drawing our lettering in the black hardcover sketchbooks we all carried. Weekend skate sessions turned into graffiti missions, and we started painting our tag names in high-profile areas along highway overpasses. Your tag was your brand, and the point was to get it up in as many places as possible. I was obsessed, and a spray can briefly became my medium of choice. But I was also trying to finish high school and was regularly getting dragged into the principal's office over allegations of vandalism. Late one night, I was chased away from a billboard down a steep grassy hill by antigraffiti cops on their all-terrain vehicles, evading them by hiding in pond water up to my neck on the side of a highway. Close calls like that cut my graffiti aspirations short.

I graduated with the class of '94 and left Connecticut for Vermont to start my first year at Green Mountain College, where my interest in snowboarding commanded more attention than higher education. I had chosen a small school in a rural state because my high school guidance counselor didn't think my short attention span would cut it at an urban university. I learned quickly that most other students spent their time in an intoxicated haze unless they were in class or on the slopes at Killington Mountain, the local ski resort.

Halfway through the first semester, I grew tired of the constant pursuit of getting fucked up. After a night of binge drinking that had me throwing up until the color drained from my face, I committed to staying sober. It was the kind of "I'll never drink again" pledge you make after waking up with a terrible hangover and learning you had earned a new, unflattering nickname the night before. I still had more than two years before I could legally drink alcohol, but I was ready to swear it off for life. Many of my hometown friends identified as being "straight edge" by this time, avoiding drugs and alcohol altogether. I hadn't wanted to label myself in high school, but I started to see the appeal.

Hardcore punk was music first made by teenagers, and most venues that traditionally hosted live performances sold alcohol. As a compromise with local bars to allow bands with younger members to perform and to let teenage fans in to see the bands play, black *X*'s were drawn on the back of their hands with a marker so the bartenders would know not to serve them. Though the original intent was to just mark the individual as underage, this ultimately helped make the letter *X* a symbol most identified with being straight edge. Fans voluntarily adopted this practice to show they didn't drink or do drugs.

First-generation American hardcore band Minor Threat were only around for three years at the start of the 1980s, but their records were considered essential listening for any hardcore-punk fan. They were one of the

GOATs—I'm talking Bill Russell of the 1962 Celtics and Bobby Orr of the 1970 Bruins Greatest of All Time status. Their music had become part of my teenage soundtrack, and, as it had for many, the idea of abstaining from drugs and alcohol was introduced to me by Ian MacKaye, the band's shaved-headed and thought-provoking vocalist with the 1981 song "Straight Edge," which inadvertently grew into a movement in the decades since, inspiring and attracting a significant following in the punk-music scene. Culturally, the narrative had been that you needed to consume alcohol and recreational drugs to relax and have fun. Ian pushed back against that mindset through his words:

> ***I'm a person just like you***
> ***But I've got better things to do***
> ***Than sit around and fuck my head***
> ***Hang out with the living dead***

and

> ***Always gonna keep in touch***
> ***Never want to use a crutch***
> ***I've got the straight edge.***

As it turned out, wanting to stay in control was a feeling that resonated with a lot of other people. That's precisely how I was beginning to feel: I no longer wanted to accept the expectation that I needed to drink or get high to fit in. There was so much I wanted to do, and I didn't need anything holding me back. I'd been listening to the band's music for years. Minor Threat's *Out of Step* album was practically given to you when you bought your first skateboard. As a young punk I'd been a fan of their aggressive sound; it took longer to appreciate the message in the lyrics.

I drifted away from the first people I'd met on campus in the freshman dorm and connected with two like-minded upperclassmen who were straight edge and fans of the same kind of blistering hardcore punk as I. Mark and Ned were from New York and New Jersey, respectively, and both had spent time going to hardcore-punk matinees at the legendary CBGB club in New York City's Lower East Side. Finding anyone at Green Mountain into punk was rare, considering there were only five hundred students—a tiny number for a college by any metric—and most were fans of jam bands like local favorites Phish and the Grateful Dead.

After classes one afternoon, Ned and I hung out with Mark in his off-campus apartment, just a few blocks from the college. The wooden stairs that led to his second-story porch were just behind the gas station that had recently replaced one of their windows after my first roommate had drunkenly punched his hand through it. While Mark tried to kick-flip a wheelless skateboard deck on the carpeted floor of his living room, I sat in front of his record player and flipped through one of the boxes of records sitting beneath it. That was one of the first things a music fan did when they visited someone else's dorm room or apartment; you looked through their record collection to see what kind of bands they were into. I pulled out Mark's copy of the Unbroken and Groundwork "split" record. Split records featured a different band on each side, which was a good way to tap into two growing audiences. Often called 45s, they were the type of smaller records you might have seen in an old-school jukebox. They can hold a few songs and in the 1980s had become popular with the hardcore-punk bands I liked because they were relatively cheap to make. This particular record had a Xerox-copy cover on light-yellow paper. It didn't look like something you'd find in a store; it looked handmade.

"I've got this one, but it has a blue cover," I said as I held it up, flipping it over to inspect the back of the record. I'd bought my copy from someone selling records out of a box at the back of a venue.

"My friend's brother put that out; his label is Bloodlink Records," Mark replied, referring to the logo on the back of the record. "The real covers took forever to arrive, so they kept making their own at Kinko's." Ah, Kinko's, the nationwide strip-mall copy center that was later bought out, becoming FedEx Office. Every punk had a friend that worked at one, and that's where they got a free hookup to print their flyers to promote live gigs. Knowing my interest in getting more involved in the punk scene, he asked, "Hey, have you ever thought of doing that? Releasing a record?"

I hadn't. It was now early 1995, and while many of my friends were starting bands, I'd never learned to play an instrument. Going back to elementary school, I'd been one of the *art* kids, so I helped my friends design demo tapes and merchandise. Contributing that way had been cool, but making a record intrigued me because I loved listening to and collecting vinyl.

In the early nineties, demand for vinyl records was fading among mainstream music fans, and most record stores had cleared their shelves of vinyl to make space for so-called superior-sounding CDs. Still, record-pressing plants stayed in business by manufacturing hip-hop and punk-rock records for indie-music entrepreneurs, a few hundred to a thousand copies at a time. Within the hardcore-punk scene, vinyl remained the preferred format with which fans curated their music collections. And making a record wasn't just the territory of the major labels; anyone could do it, even a teenage punk fan like myself, once they learned how.

"I wouldn't even know where to start," I replied as I slid the record back where I'd found it. Despite not knowing the first thing about how to make a record, I was eager to follow in the footsteps of those before me who had taken matters into their own hands, documenting their favorite unknown band with the most limited of resources. My small college town was more than an hour away from any venue whose stage welcomed the kind of bands I liked. I needed something that connected me to my hometown scene, so maybe this was it. I was interested but couldn't wrap my head around it, so Mark offered to connect me with Scott Beibin, the guy who ran Bloodlink.

I was familiar with Scott's label; a handful of Bloodlink's singles were in the milk crates that held my record collection. Mark gave me a piece of paper with Scott's home phone number in Philadelphia, and I planned to call him from the pay phone in my dorm hall, but long-distance calls in the mid-'90s were prohibitively expensive. My primary means of communication with people from out of state until then had been writing letters, rarely using the phone to talk to anyone outside my town. If you needed to, you made those calls late in the evening, when rates were lower, or on Sunday nights, when they were the cheapest. Talking on the phone to someone in a different state was a luxury reserved for people who didn't need to ask how much things cost. And when you did make a long-distance call, you were aware of every minute that passed. Because of that, when I was a kid, my parents often sat at the kitchen table and spoke into a tape recorder about what our family had been up to. They'd trade cassettes in the mail with my grandparents; listening to those was less expensive than talking on the phone.

Thankfully, Mark shared a workaround. Everyone relied on shortcuts and hacks to help level the playing field and keep pushing the hardcore-punk subculture forward. Mark told me I could call Scott using an illegally modified RadioShack tone dialer called a red box. It allowed musicians, booking agents, and indie record-label owners to communicate with others nationwide at a length and convenience that they could not otherwise afford. Before cell phones, traveling salespeople who depended on pay phones used these handheld dialers legitimately to program the long sixteen-digit numbers of their credit cards for ease in making long-distance phone calls. Instead of pulling their credit card out and punching in all the numbers every time they picked up a phone, they could hold the dialer's speaker up to the mouthpiece and touch a single button, which would play the preprogrammed touch tones that the number keys made.

This technology was hacked at some point when someone realized that replacing the crystal soldered inside changed the sound the dialer made to replicate the internal tones a pay phone made when coins were deposited. An effort known as phreaking, it allowed the user to make unlimited free phone calls, which in the mid-'90s might as well have been a superpower. The altered dialer featured three buttons that, when pushed, mimicked the sounds associated with a nickel, dime, and quarter. You dialed the phone number, and a recording told you how much to deposit for the first few minutes. Then, you held the red box up to the mouthpiece and pressed the right buttons to trick the pay phone into thinking you'd deposited the coins, and the call went through for free.

I used Mark's red box—which Scott himself had made—to call. While I'm sure Scott could tell I was unprepared for whatever would come next, that call proved incredibly helpful. As I leaned against the drably painted cinder-block wall of the dorm hallway next to the pay phone, he shared some tips and rattled off a list of contacts to use for manufacturing my first record as I wrote them down in a spiral notebook. Most important, his straightforward description of what to do gave me the confidence that this was something I could do myself.

I needed a name for my record label, and I settled on Bridge Nine. A bridge connects two places, a metaphor for what I was trying to do, as I now lived hours away from what had been most familiar to me. I learned there was already a label called Bridge Records, one that released classical music, so I kept thinking. On a drive to Boston for a show, I noticed the highway had a reflective numbered sign at every bridge, similar to a mile marker. I passed bridge 11, bridge 10, then bridge 9—my lucky number. I thought it had a nice ring to it, so Bridge Nine stuck.

Bridge Nine's premiere release was a 7-inch split record. The first band I chose to work with was Tenfold, made up of friends from my high school. They had recently kicked out their singer and wanted to release something to showcase their evolving sound and feature their new vocalist, who had put down his guitar to shout into the microphone. The other band was Sum of All Fears, who'd been playing some of the same local shows with Tenfold, and the members became tight. I met them for the first time when they performed in the basement of someone's home in the next town over from mine. The bands recorded their respective songs and gave me the tapes.

I selected a vinyl pressing plant in Nashville to manufacture the records, the same place that had pressed the first Beatles 7-inch singles in America in the early '60s. Ten boxes of records arrived at my parents' home during the summer of 1996, and I ordered pizza for friends who helped assemble them inside black-and-white fold-over record covers at the kitchen table. I hand-numbered the white dust sleeves to add a personal touch, coordinating the ink to match the color of the green and black vinyl records. We needed to prepare them for Tenfold's upcoming show at the Bristol Skate Park, a dusty warehouse filled with graffiti and skateboarding punk fans where bands performed in the middle of a half-pipe.

It took almost a year to recoup the $1,500 I had spent manufacturing that first 7-inch release, money I had saved from cutting lawns and working the counter at the local video store. Still, by 1997 I was ready to release another record, a posthumous three-song EP for Tenfold after the band had unceremoniously broken up, a fate I'd learned with the rest of the audience when they announced it onstage.

Releasing one or two records a year was more of a glorified hobby than a business, but it meant the world to me. The money earned wouldn't have covered the time I was investing, but I was creating something and connecting with people. I took out cheap little ads in fan-published photocopy and newsprint magazines known as fanzines. Because of those ads, I started exchanging handwritten letters with like-minded people from across the United States, Europe, and Asia.

Hardcore punk is a relatively small musical genre, but one with a tightly linked fan base that extends worldwide—bands have managed to tour Europe on just the strength of a demo and a good five- or six-song EP, much to the chagrin of Guitar Center employees stuck performing at the same local bars month after month. Despite being one of the hundreds of similarly sized record labels operating out of bedrooms, I had begun to tap into that audience as I sold records off my folding merch table in the back of dimly lit basements, VFW halls, and clubs.

The main objective of an indie label is to find a band you like and give them whatever you can to help them meet their potential. You put them into a studio to record their music and get their album artwork designed, and once a record is ready to be sold, you figure out how to market and distribute it. Major labels, of which there are only three (Universal, Sony, and Warner), distribute through their own sales channels. Indie labels, so-called because they are independently owned, are distributed through more unique means.

My label was literally the furthest thing from "major," so my way of getting records into people's hands at the time included consignment deals through a patchwork of stores and small distributors that only paid me months after they were sold. If I pressed 1,000 records, I'd give the band 150 copies, which they'd sell and pocket the money as their "cut." I sold some of the records through the mail, but moved most of them at local shows. My earliest releases weren't available in many stores; you had a better chance of getting a copy from me or the band directly. Distribution often involved exchanging records instead of money; I'd trade ten or twelve copies of a release to people doing the same thing as me in other cities and countries for theirs. We'd sell each other's records to expand our respective reach, a few records at a time. It wasn't much, but it was a start.

With Bridge Nine, finally, I had a sense of purpose and something that commanded my full attention, focusing my energy better than Prozac ever did.

CHAPTER 3

9 Sewall

I MOVED TO BOSTON AFTER GRADUATING COLLEGE IN 1998 WITH a fine-arts degree but no job prospects. I was drawn to the city because a lot of my hometown friends into hardcore-punk music had settled in the area; a dozen from my high school lived in the Mission Hill neighborhood by the time I arrived. Despite being welcomed by a group of familiar faces, I discovered Boston was a much larger city where people moved in more diverse circles than where I was from.

Being new to the area, I explored the city every night on my skateboard, often ending up at Tower Records, flipping through magazines and CDs because it was the only place open until midnight. If you're not familiar with Tower Records, they weren't your typical record store. They were a megastore, absolute temples to music, and this location had three floors and more than twenty-five thousand square feet of CDs, books, and videos. You could get lost in there for hours, and I would often. On every wall, large displays promoted new albums. There were hundreds throughout the store, all made by hand. Each letter had been cut out of foam core and painted, giving them a three-dimensional look. They weren't mass-market promotional items;

they were individual works of art, and Tower Records wasn't just a store, but a pop art museum for music. I needed to get a job there; it was that cool.

I walked into the Tower store with a copy of my résumé, which I'd printed on a fancy piece of expensive off-white stationery, the kind with a watermark that implied I was taking my job hunt seriously. The store's manager told me they weren't hiring and would keep my résumé on file. *Damn.* I decided to stay on his radar in case something opened up. A couple of weeks later, I mailed him some photographs of art I'd made with a few facts about myself to help me stand out from any other applicants. I continued to send something similar every few weeks until he finally gave me a call to come in for an interview. The art department was a tight crew that rarely had an opening, but someone was finally leaving, and I had been persistent enough to get a chance for the coveted spot. The interview went well, and I landed the job. It didn't pay much, but the store's culture was the selling point. It was a massive community dedicated to all things music, and I felt fortunate to count myself in the mix.

Shelves full of art supplies surrounded my desk, all crammed into a poorly lit basement room where the art department was located. The floor would vibrate every few minutes from the rumbling movement of the Green Line subway trains that slowly passed beneath us as they entered the Hynes Convention Center T station below while I made signs and window displays for popular new albums.

I enjoyed the work, but my paycheck—just an extra buck an hour over minimum wage—barely covered my rent, and I wasn't exactly in the position to launch a band's career. I wanted to do something to help me meet more people and decided to publish a small newsletter, the *Boston Hardcore & Punk Factsheet*, in a digest-size format I knew I could manage monthly. I patterned it after a fanzine I had printed in high school and had anonymously slid into lockers as my means of distribution. The first issue of the *Factsheet* came out after I'd been in the city for less than a year and featured an interview with a local band on the cover, music news, and a list of upcoming local shows. I had brief conversations with band members and didn't focus on one niche sound but attempted to include people from the entire spectrum of Boston's punk, metal, indie, and hardcore bands. I quickly jotted down answers to my questions with a pencil in a notebook while we chatted outside the venue they were playing that night. It became a dependable news source and show listing before that information was readily available online.

Every month I'd print thousands of each issue on the copiers in the basement offices of Tower Records and would fold them in half by hand. At first, I brought a stack to every show and stood outside the exit as the crowd left, handing each one out personally. Later, I added branded dispensers constructed out of the foam-core board I used to make signs at work and placed them in local record stores so there would be a consistent place to grab a copy.

I managed to print twelve issues over the course of a year, which allowed me to introduce myself to the most active contributors in the music scene and promote what they were doing. Many of these people would later reciprocate and assist my efforts in the following years as I became more of a fixture in Boston.

While I worked on the newsletter to promote what was happening in the Boston scene each month, my Bridge Nine label began representing a handful of local bands with small followings that hadn't toured much outside New England. When family friends at holiday parties heard that I was in the record business, they thought of the Grammys and shiny gold records hanging on walls. They asked if I'd met Justin Timberlake or if they could hear my bands on the radio. I hadn't, and they couldn't, unless it was late at night on some low-frequency college station at the far end of the dial.

The groups I worked with would typically pack their instruments and a couple of friends into a van to drive a state or two away to perform in a rented church hall or someone's basement. If they were lucky or well connected, they'd get a chance to open up a show in a real nightclub when a nationally known band toured through town. Any money received from ticket sales or selling a handful of T-shirts went into their gas tank or toward the next month's rent for their practice space. It was a mostly word-of-mouth scene that didn't hit the radar outside of small circles of fans.

While my roommates were watching TV and playing video games, I packed mail orders in my bedroom and brought them to the Mission Hill post office every few days to send them out. Visiting this post office was part of my weekly routine, shipping records, T-shirts, and single-page catalogs I had created by cutting and pasting the design by hand before printing them in a photocopier. I folded those around a Bridge Nine sticker and mailed them to the few dozen people that had sent a dollar bill hidden inside an envelope the previous week.

It wasn't a busy location as far as post offices went, just a small neighborhood branch with two cashiers on the street-level floor of a large apartment building. My reception on any given day depended on who was at the counter, ranging from cordial to contemptuous. I was becoming a high-volume shipper, with anywhere from twenty to thirty packages, so whoever ended up with me would have their hands full for a bit. Each of my parcels had to be individually weighed and stamped, with a customs declaration notice detailing each item inside stuck on anything traveling out of the country. I stood in line there a few times a week, usually with a skateboard by my side, balancing a stack of white plastic postal bins filled with packages.

The gentleman with the naval tattoo on his forearm didn't mind when I turned up at his station; we'd make some initial small talk, and then he could zone out and work on autopilot for the fifteen minutes it took to process my packages. The older woman counting the days until her retirement couldn't hide her frustration with me; each item on what usually produced a three- to four-foot receipt seemed a personal attack on her. She had no trouble making her displeasure known, especially when someone else with an armful of packages plugged up the other register. You could hear everyone groan when that happened as the line behind me ground to a halt.

Being short on funds forced me to get creative with promoting the label and the bands it represented. I couldn't afford much in the way of traditional advertising, so I had to look for other means to get the word out. Riding the Green Line from Mission Hill, I noticed advertisements mounted between the windows on every train. They were card-stock prints, roughly four square feet, and designed for easy insertion into the frame from below. I slid one out and took it to Tower Records to use as a template for making posters that promoted the singles for up-and-coming Boston hardcore-punk bands. I then returned to the Green Line, where I spent the rest of the evening sliding them into the frames on various trains.

I also tried to work my label's name into the surrounding environment in ways that wouldn't be so obvious. One day I noticed a billboard on the roof of a two-story retail building on Harvard Avenue in Boston's Allston neighborhood. It was a busy street, and the advertisement featuring the lasagna-loving cartoon cat Garfield promoted the dairy industry's "Got Milk?" campaign with a "9 nutrients, 9 lives" tagline. I saw an opportunity to hijack the billboard, so I printed out *BRIDGE NINE?* in the distinctive font used for "Got Milk?" and enlarged it to about eight feet wide on white paper through a copy shop where Tower Records had an account. Then, late at night, I climbed up the rusty fire escape at the back of the building with a bucket of wheat paste, a brush, and my rolled-up poster.

A single spotlight lit up the sign, so I laid my jacket over it to provide the cover of darkness. I dipped my brush into the bucket and began to spread the milky-white paste over the "Got Milk?" message. I then pressed the edge of my poster against the sticky surface, unrolling it across the billboard and completely covering the original slogan, turning it into my own marketing tool after a few minutes and brushstrokes. I spread more paste across the poster to lock it in place, and as I finished, I pulled my jacket off the light, illuminating the updated sign.

My most significant Bridge Nine "advertisement" was painted across the Charles River on the steel-plate girder Grand Junction Railroad Bridge opposite the Storrow Drive parkway behind Boston University. I had to stand on top of an eight-inch-diameter pipe that ran alongside the bridge, jutting off the side eleven feet above the river at two in the morning. Covered by decades of graffiti, the bridge was almost three hundred feet wide with six-foot-tall riveted steel panel walls on each side. More than one hundred thousand cars drove past it daily.

I gauged the distance to the river's surface by how the moon glistened on the pitch-black water below. A skateboarding friend (who'd also been a founding member of Tenfold) dropped me off in his car an hour earlier with a five-gallon bucket of white paint and a couple gallons of black paint. Over the next hour, with a six-inch broad paint roller, I wrote out "BRIDGE NINE X BHC 1999 DIY X" in four-foot bold black letters. "BHC" is an acronym for Boston Hardcore, and DIY referenced how I jumped into the label with a do-it-yourself ethic. Perhaps one of my riskier solo missions, one misstep walking on the pipe could have been the end of this story.

I slapped Bridge Nine on everything with the same obsession I'd had years earlier as a budding graffiti artist, trying to get the name in places where it would often stay up for months. The most permanent placement, however, was on my own body. Tattooing was outlawed in Massachusetts from 1962 until 2001 over health-risk fears and designated a crime against the person. During that time, the only legal option for people in Boston was to drive to New Hampshire or Rhode Island. The shop of choice for some of the more notable members of Boston's hardcore-punk scene was Art Freek, an hour south in Providence. Because most of us didn't have reliable cars, one of their artists, Mike Lussier, often drove up to Boston with his mobile kit and set up shop in someone's apartment, spending the day putting traditional-style tattoos on friends. During the summer of 1999, when a friend hosted a tattoo party at his apartment and invited me at the last minute, I had to lay on a coffee table in his living room to get a large stomach rocker as my first tattoo—"Bridge Nine" inked across my abdomen in two-inch letters. I'd only released four records by this point, but I knew it was something I wanted to do for the rest of my life.

I'd been living in Boston for a year and was still meeting new people regularly. I met Rod shortly after landing the job at Tower Records. He worked the counter at a skateboard shop a few doors down Newbury Street. A formidable guy, Rod was a short-haired, muscular, skateboard-riding metalhead with a gigantic H. R. Giger–inspired tattoo of an alien ripping out of his chest that he'd gotten as a teenager, as well as a mid-'90s-era Slayer album cover on his inner bicep. While Rod was a fan of heavy music, he wasn't a member of Boston's closely knit hardcore scene; he was more of an Ozzfest guy than a punk. But he quickly became one of my favorite people to hang out with because he was down to do *anything*. He had an infectious laugh and a warm, gap-toothed grin that reminded me of a rugged version of *MAD Magazine*'s Alfred E. Neuman mascot. I'd stop by the shop to talk about music and skateboarding when he was working. We started having regular skate sessions together at the smooth waxed-granite ledges of the empty fountain in Copley Square during our lunch breaks and after work.

Rod was also really fucking smart, having as much brain as brawn that drew comparisons to the unrecognized genius of the South Boston janitor played by Matt Damon in the film *Good Will Hunting*. An engineering student enrolled at Northeastern University, Rod worked at the skateboard shop on weekends. His side hustle was dealing marijuana and psychedelic mushrooms to college kids. He also sold mountain bikes he'd stolen from neighboring college campuses. Rod justified the wholesale theft of bicycles by giving a few to the less fortunate kids in our neighborhood, like a drug-dealing Robin Hood on a ten-speed.

When Rod and I were looking for new apartments in the summer of 1999, we decided to find one together with a couple of friends. We moved into a skinny four-story row house a few streets from where I'd been living. Rod had found the apartment and took the largest bedroom on the top floor. His laid-back skateboarding buddy from Northeastern, Seth, took the room across the hall. I grabbed one on the first floor. My friend Tim Cossar, who played guitar in the band Ten Yard Fight, took the bedroom in the basement. A friend I'd met through Tim, Wes Eisold, later took the room down the hall that shared a bathroom with mine.

The apartment was so close that I stacked everything I owned on an upside-down wooden desk on top of my skateboard and pushed it to the new apartment. It took a dozen trips as I navigated the Mission Hill streets by holding the legs of the table and putting pressure on each side to turn the corners at the intersections.

When I first moved to the neighborhood, I was warned not to keep a rental truck out front for too long. You didn't want to advertise your arrival and parade your belongings in case anyone was paying attention, intending to break in and take them at a later date. Though it was still considered dangerous, the seeds of gentrification had taken root. Despite remaining gangland elements, artists and college students who had been lured to the area by cheap rent and its proximity to schools were tipping the scale.

Houses filled with hardcore-punk fans dotted the neighborhood; among us, they were all referred to by their street address. Worm and a few guys lived at 38 Calumet, another four or five friends were at 8 Carmel, and others at 36 Cherokee. Ours was 9 Sewall—the neighborhood jewel, nicer in every way. It sat on a quiet one-way street with little traffic; a neighborhood park was next to the building that stretched to the end of the block. The TV was larger and the couches were cleaner, probably one of the perks of having a roommate with drug-dealing money.

In the corner of our living room, partially hidden by Rod's collection of hot mountain bikes, sat a large aquarium of brightly colored fish that took up an entire section of wall. One night Galle tried to feed them, sprinkling too many flakes of fish food onto the water's surface.

Rod stared at him and said, "Galle, you're going to kill my fish."

Looking over his shoulder, Galle replied, "Let 'em live a little," unaware that overfeeding could prove fatal. Rod had to skim off the extra food with a little net, and another Galle-ism was born. I've lost count of how many times I've said "Let 'em live a little" when referring to anything excessive in the years since.

Rod had a passion for gambling that synced with the rest of my crew of friends. They all ended up behind stacks of poker chips at the same Mission Hill card games late at night. Our 9 Sewall apartment became a regular hangout in the neighborhood and was one of the many places where they tried to take each other's money—that is, when they weren't away on the weekends at the casinos in Connecticut, sleeping by the pool to avoid springing for a hotel room.

While my friends were busy gambling away their cash, I sought new ways to get more of my own. Getting the word out about Bridge Nine needed more than my DIY marketing. Ultimately, the most important responsibility was finding the money to produce and promote new records. I tried going to banks, but I quickly learned they weren't giving out loans to someone like me who wanted to release punk-rock records. I had no home to refinance, no trust fund or savings to raid. I didn't even have a car to offer up as collateral. The suits on the other side of the desks stopped just short of laughing as they stared at me in my T-shirt, jeans, and sneakers while I inquired about borrowing the tens of thousands of dollars necessary to push an album. I was the furthest thing from a safe bet and would have to find the money I needed some other way.

When I first moved to Boston, I daydreamed of earning one dollar from every college student, who numbered 150,000 strong. If I could do that, I'd be set, I figured. I financed early releases making signs for some of the nightclubs on Lansdowne Street, gigs I'd landed through connections made at my Tower job. I also sold promotional posters and other items advertising albums featured at the record store on the recently launched eBay. I even sold Bridge Nine skateboards—a short-lived effort—at the shop where Rod worked. My most profitable venture at that time had been selling subculture-themed novelty bumper stickers to Hot Topic after a friend who managed one of their stores gave me the buyer's contact.

I had walked into his store late one night just before closing, and while I waited for him to count out the cash drawer, I stared at the bumper stickers for sale inside the glass counter. They were basic black-and-white stickers with boldly printed edgy phrases. I thought to myself, "I could make these." So I spent time trying to design and pitch stickers that would appeal to Hot Topic's customers. The buyer for the chain ordered the first sticker I sent, which simply stated "I Love SKA," with a black-and-white checkered heart, a pattern popular in the genre.

I didn't love ska music, but I recognized it as something fans would buy. If I could make money from something random like a novelty bumper sticker and reinvest it in the label, maybe that's how I could raise the capital I needed. It was years before crowdfunding became a viable option for artists and entrepreneurs. Even if that support had been available, I didn't have much of a crowd following me anyway. After successfully selling a few thousand of the ska stickers and thousands more of a "Big Brother Is Watching You" crime watch–eyeball parody sticker, I put the money into pressing records for two new Boston-area bands, Proclamation and the Trust. Checks from Hot Topic started to come in every other month, and it was the easiest money I'd made until that point, but it still wasn't enough.

CHAPTER 4

10.17.99

IT'S BEEN SAID THAT IT TAKES TWENTY YEARS FOR FASHIONS to return to style, and by the late 1990s at Fenway Park, wearing something that told everyone you hated the Yankees was back in vogue. Street vendors put the ubiquitous "Yankees Suck" slogan on T-shirts again and were selling them to the crowds attending Red Sox games. Their navy-blue shirts featured "Boston" arched across the chest in white-outlined red letters and "Yankees Suck" across the shoulder blades, mimicking the placement of a player's last name on the back of a jersey. The slogan arched over the number 21, notably last worn by Red Sox pitching ace Roger Clemens. After twelve dominating seasons, Clemens departed from Boston in 1997 for a more lucrative deal with the Toronto Blue Jays, before being traded to the Yankees. He curried no favor with Sox fans, and his debut with Boston's rivals in the Bronx was considered blasphemy. Another Boston hero had bitten the dust.

In the fall of 1999, vendors waved the T-shirts to the crowds headed to watch the Red Sox take on the Blue Jays. The large number on the back of their shirts earned the vendors the nickname "the 21-ers" among my friends.

They rented sidewalk space from the owner of a subterranean sock store one block from Fenway Park in the highly trafficked Kenmore Square, where Commonwealth Avenue and Beacon Street intersect, abutting Boston University and home to a variety of restaurants and retailers. Kenmore Square is visible from most points in Boston due to the enormous six-story Citgo oil-company sign perched on top of a building there. One of the more iconic additions to Boston's skyline, the red triangle on a white square contained five miles' worth of neon tubing (replaced with LEDs in 2005), and the red, white, and blue lights that blink intermittently at night make it one of the city's most recognizable landmarks.

Thousands of fans walked through Kenmore Square in the shadow of the Citgo sign on their way to the stadium. The sidewalk came alive around every game. Street drummers sat on multiple corners, pounding away on sets of five-gallon white buckets like they played in the band Aerosmith, soliciting tips from Red Sox fans who walked by. Scalpers stood along the sidewalk, holding pairs of tickets and calling out, "Buying, selling, trading, upgrading!" to fans trying to catch a last-minute entry into a game. A river of opportunity outfitted in Red Sox jerseys, hats, jackets, and T-shirts flowed by. The 21-ers had pulled together a group of friends who helped them sell the shirts, earning a commission from each one sold. More than enough people were looking to buy them, allowing their ranks to grow. The 21-ers enjoyed what seemed like a monopoly, attracting fans and reeling in money hand over fist while selling their T-shirts for twenty dollars apiece.

This particular Tuesday, my friend Worm, who sold concessions inside Fenway Park, first noted the vendors' success on his way to work. He normally entered the stadium from the right-field entrance at Gate B, which was on the side facing Mission Hill, but he'd been hanging out on Newbury Street before the game. On his walk to Gate E at Fenway Park's main entrance, he had to pass right by the 21-ers and saw all the action.

When he wasn't dressed in the distinctive yellow baseball jersey of a Fenway Park concession vendor, hawking snacks to Red Sox fans from the concrete stairs between the rows of bleachers, Worm was an active member of the Boston hardcore-punk music scene like the rest of us. No stranger to the do-it-yourself ethic that the scene fostered, Worm was, like our mutual friend Galle, a part-time organizer of punk-rock shows in church basements and legion halls. Worm babbled with a distinct lisp that was almost impossible for our friends not to mimic when retelling a story that included him, and it seemed he was always up to something worthy of a tale after the fact.

On game days, most people walking to Fenway Park saw the 21-ers only as a bunch of college-aged street vendors selling novelty shirts to fans, but Worm saw dollar signs. The 21-ers held their T-shirts for sale backward over their heads, drawing attention to the "Yankees Suck" phrase arched across the shoulders. They were out on the street before and after games, standing on milk crates and trading T-shirts for cash to a sea of fans and making more money than Worm was selling ice cream during the game—and a lot more than I was taking home from Tower Records. Worm did the math: two colors of ink on both sides of a navy-blue tee ran, what, five or six bucks each? From his experience touring with bands and helping sell their merch, Worm knew the shirts the 21-ers sold were unnecessarily expensive to print. The attention-catching phrase was almost hidden on the back yet sold for a hefty profit. It also had "Boston" printed across the chest, a detail that didn't appeal to fans of the other teams visiting Fenway who also shared a mutual hatred of the Yankees. Worm knew he could make a better "Yankees Suck" tee for as little as two dollars each, and since most of our friends were looking to make extra money, he'd have plenty of help moving them. Printing the slogan boldly with navy-blue ink on the front of a much cheaper white shirt, he could sell them for half the price that the 21-ers were asking and to a larger number of people.

At the time, the Red Sox were facing elimination by the Yankees in their first postseason matchup since 1978, barely capturing hope with Red Sox pitching ace Pedro Martínez on the mound. He gave New York and hometown hero turned rival Roger Clemens their only American League Championship Series loss during Game Three. Game Four fell on Sunday, October 17, 1999, the same night as the sold-out final performance by my roommate Tim's band, Ten Yard Fight. Ten Yard Fight was a Boston hardcore band made up of friends and had been a prominent force during the mid-'90s East Coast hardcore-punk revival.

The band formed in Boston's Mission Hill neighborhood in 1995, and it was initially a tongue-in-cheek project inspired by a fondness of 1980s-era straight-edge hardcore-punk music. They took their name in jest from a gridiron-themed video game published by Nintendo in 1985. Ten Yard Fight's football aesthetic was inspired more by collegiate fashion, appropriating varsity jackets and Nike sneakers. The influence of other Boston-area bands was evident in their look as well as their sound—namely, Society System Decontrol (SSD), Department of Youth Services (DYS), and Slapshot.

Ten Yard Fight's songs referenced playing football with lyrics like: "You turned in your helmet, you fumbled the ball / You lost the edge man, you're gonna fall." The band's members weren't sports fans—and singing about football was more of a gimmick than anything else. But fans embraced them, building a loyal following in the scene. In most cities, fans of punk music and fans of sports did not mix well, leaving a big gap between the two. The band 7 Seconds from Reno, Nevada, wrote a song titled "I Hate Sports" in 1980. The Dead Kennedys from San Francisco regularly took jabs at jock culture on their albums. That wasn't the case in Boston, where hardcore and punk bands have expressed support for the city's professional sports teams for years. Being a punk and liking sports here gets a pass. These days the Celtic-punk band Dropkick Murphys straddles that line the proudest: you can hear their music played inside every stadium, and their song "Time to Go" is a love letter to the Boston Bruins hockey team.

Ten Yard Fight released multiple records, toured all over the United States and Europe, and did more than they ever expected in the time it took for the average Boston University student to earn a degree. Four years came and went, and by early 1999, the band felt they had done everything they wanted to do. During that time, stylistic shifts in the hardcore-punk music scene began as new bands emerged, continuing a pattern that had developed over the previous fifteen years. Like most art, music often reacts to whatever had come before it. In the early 1980s, straight-edge hardcore was a response to the self-destructive attitude of punk and its "Live Fast, Die Young" credo of the late 1970s. Bands like Washington, DC's Minor Threat and Boston's SSD and DYS wrote songs that championed a drug- and alcohol-free lifestyle over even faster music. By the mid-'80s, many of hardcore punk's first wave of bands disbanded, and those that stayed together slowed down their sound, becoming more influenced by hard rock (and the desire to show that they could actually play their instruments with more complex songs). But new bands like Boston's Slapshot and New York City's Youth of Today were starting to bring hardcore back to the rawer elements of its earliest form.

Hardcore-punk music's growing wave through the late '80s crested in 1991 as Nirvana burst into the mainstream with their hit song "Smells Like Teen Spirit." Many of the genre's most innovative artists moved on to create new bands and find commercial success as the hardcore-punk underground was mined by major label A&R (artist and repertoire) execs looking for the next big thing in youth subculture. Dissatisfied with where the scene and sound had gone, Ten Yard Fight found themselves in the same place Slapshot had a decade earlier and were now ready to call it quits.

Ten Yard Fight booked their own send-off show at Karma Club on the bar-laden side of Lansdowne, the street bordering Fenway Park's left field.

I don't think anyone realized it would end up positioning more than a thousand hardcore-punk fans head-on with a stadium worth of baseball fans walking into Fenway Park.

Friends of the band created unofficial merchandise to commemorate their final performance. My contribution was a poster that featured a collage of photos of the band that I'd stenciled with the date of the show, "10.17.99," using bright-orange spray paint. I'd been inspired by a Nike sneaker campaign plastered over subway stations that spring, advertising the 103rd annual Boston Marathon. I first used the stencil as part of my guerrilla marketing effort to help promote the show by painting it across sidewalks close to the venue and saw this as a way of letting people frame my tribute to a band that many people were sad was calling it a day.

Worm took the opportunity to pay respect by making his own "Yankees Suck" shirt. The slogan was printed prominently on the front, and "TYF" and the date of the show were on the back. It was designed by our friend from New Jersey Geoff Dagostino, who printed T-shirts for many of the bands we knew. The lettering was inspired by the logo of the late-'80s hardcore-punk cut-and-paste fanzine *Boiling Point*, with YANKEES printed in blue letters above a blue rectangle with SUCK knocked out of it in contrasting white letters. The Berthold City typeface was chosen purposefully, as the band SSD had used it seventeen years earlier on the album *The Kids Will Have Their Say*. SSD had been the architects of Boston's first wave of hardcore punk and were acknowledged by all as having laid the foundation of DIY Boston hardcore music as we knew it.

The Ten Yard Fight show started in the afternoon after a dominating 13–1 win by the Red Sox over the Yankees the night before. Worm's shirt was an instant hit. Any that weren't given to friends or sold at the show were snapped up by an excited Red Sox fan base outside of the club as they headed to the game, flung over shoulder after shoulder as Worm worked to keep up with the demand. The excitement of the crowds was palpable after the team had dominated the night before, keeping hopes alive of the team finally breaking the Curse of the Bambino.

Ten Yard Fight's send-off had all the elements to make the evening legendary. Even the will-call ticket list arriving late contributed to the exciting atmosphere. The venue couldn't open the doors on time, so people continued to line up outside. A crowd of more than a thousand attendees extended for blocks down the street, taking up the entire width of the sidewalk. Fans began climbing the small trees along the sidewalk and jumping from them onto willing participants in line in an attempt to crowd surf hours before the first band of the night played even a note of music.

The horde of Ten Yard Fight fans didn't look out of place across the street from the Red Sox fans ready to watch a showdown with their rivals from the Bronx. Chants of "Yankees suck" broke out from both sidewalks, directed at New York fans repping the team's distinctive pinstripes and hats headed down Lansdowne Street.

This show would be *the* hardcore-punk bill of the year in the city, and it almost didn't happen. Because the band had booked the show themselves, they needed to supply an insurance policy with a million dollars of coverage, but they couldn't afford the premium. They solved this problem by submitting a bogus liability insurance certificate. The show was on, and they just needed to pray that no one got hurt. Despite cutting their teeth in smaller VFW halls, the band had chosen a higher-profile, larger venue that typically featured hip-hop and dance music to accommodate their many fans, some traveling from as far as Japan to send them off. It was a true DIY event, just on a bigger scale. All of the supporting bands on the bill were close friends, each with a history with Ten Yard Fight, having toured together or even having shared members at one point. Reach the Sky, Bane, and In My Eyes all hailed from the Greater Boston area, while their Equal Vision Records labelmates Floorpunch drove up from New Jersey to play a few songs.

Instead of contracting the security detail to the heavy-handed, yellow shirt–wearing "professional" bouncers commonly employed by bigger venues in Boston and Cambridge, it was turned over to scene veterans. Ten Yard Fight wanted people who understood the scene to do the security detail to ensure that fans dancing and stage diving during the band's final performance wouldn't get dragged away and thrown out into the street by misunderstanding flashlight-wielding bouncers. What could be perceived as chaos by an outsider was just a coordinated eruption of energy by fans. The blurred line between the band and the audience had become an established part of the hardcore-punk culture.

In the early 1980s as the hardcore music scene was only just beginning to form, when asked by *Boston Rock* magazine about violence at shows, SSD guitarist and founding member Al Barile replied, "I see no violence in the scene at all. The same people that say there is violence in our scene would complain about pro football and hockey being violent." This statement came from someone who had regularly performed with a guitar covered in Boston Bruins stickers. While violence did later become an element in the scene, it was not in the form of fans moshing or jumping off the stage onto each other.

When the Karma Club doors finally opened, the venue quickly filled to over capacity, and the evening became a defining moment for those lucky to have made it in and those who missed the chance. Fans entering walked past a line of tables displaying the band's T-shirts and merchandise. I had my spray-painted posters for sale alongside the handful of Bridge Nine T-shirts and 7-inch singles, selling out of them quickly.

Each performance worked the crowd up, and the temperature rose inside the venue until it was oppressively hot. The concert was the end of a musical era for many. The '90s were coming to a close. The Y2K bug, a concern that computer systems worldwide would stop working at midnight on New Year's Eve because of a glitch that wouldn't let them recognize the year 2000, dominated the headlines, stoking end-of-the-world conspiracies.

In addition, my core group of friends in Mission Hill—who had been brought together through a mutual affinity for fast, loud music while abstaining from drinking and drugs as part of the straight-edge hardcore-punk subculture—was starting to fracture. A few who had spent the latter half of the '90s going to hardcore shows and stage diving with bold black *X*'s drawn on their hands were now in their early twenties and hanging with new friends at bars on the weekends. With one of the two most prominent Boston straight-edge bands ending their run and the other going out in a similarly celebrated fashion the following year, the momentum this current wave of straight-edge hardcore had gained from the mid-1990s was starting to wane.

But Ten Yard Fight's last show gave birth to a holiday where fans could celebrate straight edge. Onstage, Sweet Pete, the vocalist of the band In My Eyes, proclaimed between songs that October 17 would forever be known as Edge Day and that he would celebrate it "from now until doomsday," which if you believed the hype over Y2K was just two months away.

The audience exploded while Ten Yard Fight played for more than an hour, finishing their set with the first song they'd ever released, "First and Ten." The more than one thousand fans in attendance sang every word and met the final notes with celebratory air horns, confetti, and colorful Silly String flying through the air. People singing along overran the stage, their shirts soaked with sweat and clinging to their bodies. Many crowd members surfed across the top of the audience while people chanted, "Ten Yard Fight! Ten Yard Fight! Ten Yard Fight!" over the music's last notes.

In stark contrast across the street inside Fenway Park, there was no opportunity for celebration, and the mood was decisively somber. The Yankees held a one-run lead over the Red Sox for most of the game but blew it open in the top of the ninth inning, adding six more runs. The Sox had their eighth inning cut short over a bad call by the umpire, giving credit to the Yankees for tagging out a base runner when the second baseman's glove hadn't come within a foot of him. After another extremely close call where

Red Sox shortstop Nomar Garciaparra was thrown out at first base when everyone except the umpire thought he was safe, the crowd started to turn. Red Sox manager Jimy Williams protested the botched call and was thrown out of the game. Fans chanted, "Bullshit, bullshit, bullshit," and threw objects from the stands. The umpires had to clear the field for the safety of the players, and the game was delayed for eight minutes until cooler heads prevailed. The Red Sox ended up losing 9–2.

The fate of Boston's baseball season was decided the next night in a tense Game Five. The Yankees invited Babe Ruth's eighty-three-year-old daughter, Julia Ruth Stevens, to throw out the ceremonial first pitch in a nod to the Curse that bore her father's name. The single run the Red Sox put on the board in the bottom of the eighth was trampled by the six driven home by the Yankees. Boston was eliminated from contention, and the Yankees went on to win the 1999 World Series. The Red Sox had come close but, once again, hadn't gotten close enough.

CHAPTER 5

Y2K

AS THE GUY WITH A LABEL, I WAS IN THE BUSINESS OF SELLING records, but in person, I had just been casually moving them at punk shows. A few here, a few there. The sales added up, but I'd never had a line of people waiting to buy anything.

At Fenway Park, however, what I saw during the 1999 season was a completely different story. People stood one after another, awaiting their chance to give the 21-ers their money. Lines extended in every direction, and the sales didn't stop. The 21-ers were seemingly getting rich, and Worm had sold out of everything he brought to Ten Yard Fight's last show. It was eye-opening for all of us to see how fervent Boston fans were when it came to the rivalry with the Yankees. But by the time we realized it, the season was over, and the Yankees were World Series winners once again.

Since I'd been the guy in the neighborhood known for making and selling things, Worm and I connected after the success of his shirt. The lucrative sticker sales I'd enjoyed through Hot Topic starting in 1997 had peaked in '98 and fizzled out by the summer of 1999, and I was looking for a new source of revenue. We both knew Worm had grabbed only a tiny piece of a much bigger opportunity, so we brainstormed ways to make the most of it the following season because one thing was certain: come April, upwards of thirty-eight thousand people would be visiting Fenway Park for every single game. I decided to order a thousand bumper stickers and buttons with the "Yankees Suck" slogan on them.

Like most people originally from central Connecticut, I had grown up as a Red Sox fan, despite being the son of transplanted New Yorkers. The state is split down the middle concerning its sports allegiance: Hartford County, where I was from, and points north rep Boston, while New Haven County and points south overwhelmingly support the Yankees. My last trip inside Fenway Park had been with my dad well over a decade earlier, when I was just ten years old, during the ill-fated 1986 "ball between Buckner's legs" season. Shortly after, I traded my baseball cards for a skateboard, as my interest in team sports waned. I quit playing baseball when my teammates started taking it seriously and instead focused my energy on learning how to ollie on my skateboard in my driveway while listening to faster and heavier music. When Worm and I began talking, I could have named maybe two players on the Red Sox roster, and the only thing I knew about the Yankees was that I still had a Don Mattingly rookie card—one of their 1980s MVPs—in a box of old baseball cards somewhere, but that wasn't the point. If I could sell ska stickers to ska fans, I could sell baseball stickers to baseball fans.

For New Year's Eve, most of the 9 Sewall crew and the rest of the Mission Hill punk houses scored cheap plane tickets and went to Las Vegas to celebrate the coming of the new millennium. The hype going into 2000 was palpable, and the Vegas Strip sounded like one of the wildest places to celebrate, precisely what we wanted. The group split between those heavily into gambling and those just along for the trip. It was strictly on a budget; this crew had no high rollers. Twelve of us crammed into one hotel room, and most slept on the floor—which was fine; like any road trip with a band, we all slept on the floor and used a balled-up sweatshirt as a pillow. At least here, there was a plush carpet instead of the hardwood found in the houses where we would normally crash on tour. Punk houses didn't typically have carpets; those made it harder to clean up the spills.

As midnight approached, we stood along the sidewalk in front of the Paris Las Vegas Hotel & Casino, the most recent addition to the Vegas Strip. Hundreds of thousands of revelers were there to welcome the new year, but it wasn't the absolute chaos we had anticipated; Y2K-bug fears had kept people away who otherwise would have been there. The festive atmosphere in the streets had some people climbing up above the sidewalks for better views or to make a spectacle of themselves. In the minutes before the clock struck midnight, we watched a man climb to the top of a streetlight as if shimmying up a palm tree. He caught the attention of almost everyone at the crowded intersection around us. He looped his arm over the part of the pole that branched out to the signal lights and started pumping his fist in the air, to the crowd's delight. He then balanced over the pole on his stomach and stretched out as if flying before pulling himself onto it. Hundreds of people cheered as he held on and basked in the glory of conquering the light. With both legs draped over the sides, he squatted down and started to pull his body out over the street toward the end of the lamp as people laughed and applauded. He was quickly twenty feet above the crowd as he inched over the intersection. As someone who'd spent a good chunk of my youth jumping off high stages into crowds at hardcore-punk shows, I wasn't sure what he was thinking. There weren't enough people below to break his fall, which probably wouldn't make a difference from that height.

We all watched as he navigated his legs around the first signal light; you could tell his goal was to reach the end. Who knew what he'd do at that point, but he was slowly working his way to it. He continued to slide toward the next obstacle: a closed-circuit security camera pointed down the Strip, the kind you pass beneath while the yellow light turns red, hoping it doesn't capture the moment. As he grabbed the side of the camera to try to work his way around it, he touched an exposed wire, causing sparks to fly. His whole body stiffened, and he tipped over and fell headfirst to the pavement below. If the electric jolt didn't immediately kill him, the fall surely did. People screamed in horror as his crumpled body lay still in the street, with the crowd going from celebratory to shocked in seconds, just as cheers from farther away signaled the new year was upon us. The paramedics arrived as people dispersed, but nothing could be done. He was the first fatality of the evening. It sucked all of the celebration out of the area. This guy had been caught up in the moment, and in the next, his life was over. As a snowboarder we used the term *Kodak courage* when someone did an especially dangerous trick to get the attention of a crowd when it was being recorded. Pushing yourself like that didn't always work out and hadn't for this guy. The image of him toppling over kept replaying in my head. It happened so quickly and was a not so subtle suggestion to avoid unnecessary risks, something I had struggled with myself.

The weekend in Vegas had been a bonding trip for Worm, Rod, and many of my Mission Hill friends. Rod may have been the newest addition to the crew, but he was an alpha who controlled any room he entered, and my friends looked up to him. He was the one who often took risks first, letting others line up behind him. Rod connected with Worm through a mutual love of poker, while my interests were elsewhere. When they gambled that winter, I was spending time with Elisabeth or out of town for hardcore shows pushing my label. That separation led to Worm picking things up with Rod about returning to Fenway for the 2000 season.

Worm then recruited two more friends he'd been playing cards with. There was Jamey, who'd been nicknamed Mr. Awesome. He was probably the best-looking of all of us, but in an *American Psycho* sort of way, walking with the same confidence and cracking the same smile as serial killer Patrick Bateman. The other was Rusty, who'd helped Worm sell shirts outside Ten Yard Fight's final show. He was a straight-edge hardcore fan from Newport Beach attending college in Boston. His father was an attorney who, it was rumored, had bought the apartment building Rusty was living in as an investment. Any side hustles Rusty had were strictly for the thrill of it.

Worm picked his team, and they planned to push his T-shirt when the Red Sox returned that spring and not bother with the smaller items I had proposed. I felt slighted over being left out, but the "Yankees Suck" economy predated us all, and there were no formal stakes. This was a new gold rush with more than enough opportunity to go around after seeing how much cash fans were dropping at Fenway Park. I knew I needed to stay in on the action so I could funnel money into the label. I let Worm and Rod know I planned to sell the "Yankees Suck" stickers I'd ordered, which they welcomed, since we wouldn't be in direct competition. Behind the scenes, we would be operating separately, but to the rest of the world, we'd be a united front hawking our "Yankees Suck" merch.

CHAPTER 6

American Nightmare

MY ROOMMATE TIM WAS TEN YARD FIGHT'S GUITARIST FOR A short time. He appeared only on their final record, released months before the band decided to call it quits, and the experience motivated him to start something new right away. Ben Chused, Ten Yard Fight's drummer, initially jammed with him in the basement of our apartment, but other commitments kept him from doing more. And Wes Eisold, who'd been in a band with Tim years earlier in Portland, Maine, joined on vocals. He'd been a roadie for Ten Yard Fight but spent more time violently swinging his arms in the mosh pit while the band performed than actually loading anything from the van to the venue and back. Wes coined the new band's name, American Nightmare, inspired by the title of a Misfits song. Tim and Wes recruited two guys they met on tour who'd recently moved to Boston from Northern California: Jesse Van Diest and Azy Relph. Another Maine friend, Zach Wilson, rounded out the band. By November 1999, American Nightmare had its first practice.

Starting a band in Boston as they had, entirely of people from outside of Massachusetts, was common. The city is home to more than one hundred colleges and universities, so new people move into the area at the end of every summer. That's a big part of why the city's music scene remains so vibrant and diverse. The annual migration typically starts with some unfortunate out-of-state family in a U-Haul, ignoring the signs prohibiting tall trucks on Storrow Drive, the parkway that runs along the Boston side of the Charles River where I painted the railroad bridge. This misstep almost always results in blocking or hitting the first low bridge they encounter. Best case, they stop in time and screw up traffic for only an hour; worst case, they've peeled off the top of their rental truck like a can of sardines—something that happens so frequently it has become known as getting *storrowed.*

The word was getting out that Tim started a new project. Fans already sorely missed Ten Yard Fight; accounts of their final show were spread by those lucky to have made it into the sold-out event. Tim was still interested in writing aggressive music, and the sound was getting heavier. Wes introduced the most significant element to the group: his dark, reflective, and emotional lyrics centered around personal struggles, isolation, and hopelessness. He drew more inspiration from British rock bands like Joy Division and the Smiths than the first- and second-generation hardcore bands commonly cited as influences at this time. Wes was more introspective than the rest of us, using a pen to articulate his thoughts and emotions.

For the band's visual aesthetic, there would be no bold collegiate fonts frequently used by bands labeled as youth-crew hardcore, a tag attached to Ten Yard Fight. They wouldn't design T-shirts with live performance photos of Wes or Tim framed by lyrics on the back, a genre staple. No colorful fabrics would be used if they could avoid it. American Nightmare offered most of its early merchandise in just one option: black. And to further distance themselves from what had connected Tim and Wes just months earlier, there would be no reference to Ten Yard Fight. No "featuring ex-members of" on marketing stickers or flyers to promote their shows; no acknowledgment of the band that had brought Tim to prominence. That was founding guitarist

John Lacroix, drummer Ben Chused, and vocalist Anthony "Wrench" Moreschi's band. Tim purposefully wanted to introduce his new project without people thinking it was supposed to be Ten Yard Fight: Part Two.

Tim attended a local communications college and had access to a free recording studio, so six weeks after Ten Yard Fight's final show, American Nightmare recorded a four-song demo. He used the session to fulfill an assignment for class with a partner more familiar with hip-hop than hardcore punk, and the band wasn't happy with what they considered a rushed first effort. Because of this, they decided to scrap the demo. Anticipation was growing for this first post–Ten Yard Fight band, but Tim and Wes wanted to wait and deliver something they felt was worthy.

After they went back into the studio for another go at recording their demo and were satisfied with the result, the band was ready to get on a stage in front of people. They booked their first two shows in Portland, Maine, and Washington, DC, respectively—places Wes had most recently lived. They'd open for In My Eyes, a band composed of friends from Mission Hill with a national following and a brand-new album out on Revelation Records. Right Brigade, featuring my hometown friend Jesse Standhard on vocals, was also on the bill. Jesse had first played bass in Tenfold, and *Stand Hard* was the fanzine and record label he had started just before mine. As is customary in the punk-music scene, what he *did* replaced his last name, becoming his identity. He released a few records and cassettes for our friends' bands but lacked motivation, and even he would tell you he wasn't very good at keeping up with the responsibility of running a label. Instead of putting his band's new record out himself, Right Brigade's split 7-inch with Boston punks A Poor Excuse would be available from me and Bridge Nine that weekend.

American Nightmare and I piled into a rented minivan and drove north to the State Street Church in Portland. They opened the show and played for fewer than ten minutes. If you blinked, you missed it, but the entire room erupted from the start of the first distorted guitar notes. Friends who had made the trip from Boston began moshing in front of the stage, pushing each other and opening a large space in the center of the dance floor that became a familiar blur of swinging arms and legs. Fans had highly anticipated this first performance, and the band delivered. Their short set featured three of the songs from their demo, and they closed with a cover of "The Crowd" by Operation Ivy, a Berkeley, California, punk band. Wes spoke briefly from the stage, directing people to buy the other bands' merch and apologizing for not having more songs.

We then made the nine-hour drive south to DC, pit-stopping in Connecticut to sleep at my parents' house for the night. Conditions in the van were tight: three of us spent the entire drive lying flat on the instrument road cases and boxes of merchandise while staring at the ceiling of the minivan just inches away. It felt more like getting our bodies scanned by an MRI machine than heading out of state to a performance, but minivans cost half as much to rent as the more commonly used twelve-passenger vans; it was what a new band traveling to their first two shows could afford.

At each show, I operated a real-time manufacture-on-demand service, standing behind their merch table while I dubbed the band's demo tapes on a dual-cassette boom-box stereo. The covers were cut out with scissors and folded by hand, before each cassette was inserted into its hard plastic case. The band had already begun writing new songs and wanted an opportunity to rerecord the four that had appeared on the demo. I'd never seen people respond so enthusiastically for a brand-new band like this before. Something special was clearly happening, and I wanted to be a part of whatever they did next, so I offered to release their debut record on Bridge Nine. American Nightmare was the first band I would work with that was willing to tour beyond our local music scene. There were no contracts or significant cash advances; we shook hands and agreed to figure it out together.

Out of respect for the label that had released most of Ten Yard Fight's catalog, Tim mailed them a copy of the demo for consideration. Fortunately for me, that label, Equal Vision Records, passed on the chance to sign the band. It wasn't a surprise because even American Nightmare's second recording attempt was still rough, and you needed to catch them live to understand their potential. Plus, many of the more prominent independent record labels like theirs, who'd spent the 1990s releasing genre-defining albums by hardcore-punk bands, were now looking at decidedly more financially viable metal and indie artists. It left many up-and-coming bands without the financial backing and support enjoyed by those who came before them.

American Nightmare was excited to get their new songs pressed on vinyl. They chose a new recording studio; this time, the soundboard would be competently manned by Kurt Ballou, a rising recording engineer and the celebrated guitarist of the hardcore-punk band Converge. In addition, Jacob Bannon, Converge's vocalist and a highly regarded visual artist, was recruited to design the EP's artwork. Between this respected duo and all the recording and manufacturing expenses, it not only would cost a fair amount to give American Nightmare the push it needed, but also required a fair amount of knowledge of the business.

And that was the rub.

There was no formal training on how to start and run a record label, at least not when I needed it the most. To educate myself, I found a few books on the topic, but they were written assuming the reader had access to greater resources than I did. It wasn't like the inner workings of an independent record label were a code that was impossible to crack: I just needed something or someone that could spell it out for me in a way that I could understand.

I'd only put the Bridge Nine logo on six releases by this point, and the effort needed to push the bands correlated with how much they were willing to tour, which until now had been minimal. I was just expected to get the records manufactured and make sure they were available from a few of the bigger mail-order companies and at a handful of stores. Thankfully, the eighteen-location Newbury Comics chain was locally headquartered, which was where most people in the Boston area shopped for new vinyl records. Newbury Comics was the original Boston punk record store and had expanded all over the Greater Boston area, and making your DIY releases easily available was just a phone call and a consignment deal away. The store was cofounded in 1978 by Mike Dreese, who went on to start the Modern Method Records label in the early 1980s. Mike released records with SSD, DYS, and the Freeze, among many others, and also notably put out the *This Is Boston, Not L.A.* compilation LP, which is an almost-perfect time capsule of the Boston hardcore-punk class of 1982, minus the notable absence of SS Decontrol. So having a retailer with as large of a reach as Newbury Comics had, with a rich history in the local punk scene, was a benefit almost exclusive to Boston.

I needed someone to show me how to take the next step, in much the same way that an aspiring tattooer must find an experienced artist to apprentice under because there were no classes on tattooing. I'd been mostly blind to my inadequacies running a label, gleaning insight from others here and there. But you can fake it for only so long until you need to actually make it. Now that I'd committed to releasing American Nightmare's record, the stakes dramatically increased. I didn't know where to even begin looking for a mentor. But then one came to me. His name was Rama Mayo, owner of Big Wheel Recreation, the *it* record label in Boston at the turn of the century. We didn't know each other well, but we lived a few streets apart and had quite a few friends in common. Big Wheel had most notably worked with artists like Jimmy Eat World, Piebald, Braid, and even Ten Yard Fight, having pressed their six-song debut as the label's third release in 1996 when I was releasing my first.

Rama, a punk-rock show promoter and entrepreneur, started his label with a friend in 1994 in his bedroom at 38 Calumet, just a few years before

Worm called the same address home and before it became the title of a song by the indie-rock band Jejune. He spent the next five years building Big Wheel, his first releases documenting music made by roommates and friends pressed on a series of color-vinyl 7-inch singles.

Like me, he had followed the same indie-label road map, a path forged more than a decade earlier by the first generation of hardcore-punk labels like Dischord Records from Washington, DC; SST Records from Long Beach, California; and X Claim! and Taang Records from here in Boston. Rama was closing in on his twentieth release by the time he and I met at a party.

Rama had lived with members of Ten Yard Fight and was familiar with my guerrilla advertising to promote the band's final show. A fan of nontraditional marketing, he appreciated the efforts I had been making and offered me a job assisting Big Wheel Recreation and other priority labels under the Lumberjack Distribution umbrella. Lumberjack was a Toledo, Ohio–based independent music distributor responsible for getting Big Wheel releases into record stores nationwide. They were looking for someone to help solicit titles from Lumberjack-distributed labels to Caroline Distribution, a major label–level distributor owned by Universal and the conduit to big-box music retailers like Tower Records, FYE, and Sam Goody. At the same time, Lumberjack handled the smaller mom-and-pop accounts. Caroline didn't want to deal directly with a hundred different indie labels like Big Wheel, so Lumberjack became the pipeline that channeled them. Rama thought I could be the guy to help manage that relationship.

I was excited by the opportunity, but the job had a hitch: it didn't come with an actual paycheck. Compensation would be a monthly $1,000 credit at a pressing plant where Lumberjack had terms. It would help me pay to press the records I released, but I was on my own to cover living expenses. In hindsight, it sounds like a terrible deal, but the benefit at the time was twofold.

First, Bridge Nine would become a distributed label through Lumberjack, a coveted opportunity because exclusive distribution deals were rare and hard to secure, and I didn't yet have the track record to earn one on my own. And second, I'd now receive personal guidance from someone with the experience and insight I desperately needed. Rama was doing his own thing on his terms and had positioned himself exactly where I hoped to be someday.

I left my job at Tower Records and went from being a basement-dwelling window artist to a marketing director assisting one of Boston's most exciting record labels. Within days, we were all in a car headed to New York City, where I was introduced to the Caroline executives at their Manhattan headquarters.

I still didn't have much money. At most, I had a few extra bucks in my pocket. I had been dipping my finger into a roommate's can of hair-shaping pomade every morning for weeks to put off buying my own a little longer. I traveled everywhere by skateboard, and eating out meant grabbing a cheap burrito, usually at the spot in Kenmore Square where a friend worked because he passed most of them over the counter free of charge.

But the first game of the baseball season was around the corner.

When my "Yankees Suck" stickers and buttons arrived, I showed them to Elisabeth.

"You're going to do what with these?" she asked.

"I'm going to go to Fenway Park when the baseball season starts to sell these to Red Sox fans," I replied, holding the stickers up closer to her, the shiny black ink reflecting a little bit of the overhead light in her room as I motioned with them.

"Are you allowed to do that?" she asked.

"I don't know, but there are a lot of other people already out there selling stuff," I responded. I wasn't sure what to expect, but knew I had to give it a shot. Growing up a punk taught me many lessons I applied daily, notably the tried-and-true "do things first, and if necessary, ask for forgiveness later." Got a good idea? Run with it. Start with whatever means you have, and then build off that. Doors stay closed around you until you make a move. If my gut feeling about the potential at Fenway Park was correct, I wouldn't have anything to worry about.

CHAPTER 7

Disruption

TUESDAY, APRIL 11, 2000. OPENING DAY OF THE 2000 BASEBALL season in Boston came with additional pomp and circumstance as it was the one-hundredth home opener for the Red Sox since their first back in 1901. As part of the new wave of hungry vendors preparing to peddle "Yankees Suck" products in the streets, I left my apartment with a jacket over my hooded sweatshirt. It was cold enough out that I could see my breath. There had been forecasts of early-April snow in Boston, and the temperature wouldn't rise above forty-five degrees before 1:00 p.m., when the game started.

I walked just beyond the Cask 'n Flagon restaurant across from Fenway Park's Gate E entrance, where Rod and a few friends had gathered, white cardboard boxes filled with freshly printed T-shirts at their feet. Rod smiled and nodded. Worm was away touring in Europe as a roadie for In My Eyes, who were supporting the legendary New York hardcore band the Cro-Mags, and wouldn't be around for another few weeks.

The game was in its final innings and would be over soon. I looked at Rusty and asked, "Does it ever get this cold in April in California?"

"Fuck this weather, dude," Rusty replied as he pulled the zipper of his jacket up higher. A couple of the other guys laughed.

I swung my backpack off my shoulder and opened it. Inside were tightly packed envelopes full of bumper stickers and a handmade sign with the sticker design and two-dollar price point printed boldly on both sides and a wooden paint stirrer wrapped with black duct tape for the handle.

The Sox had started their season on the road and had spent the week losing the last few games before returning to Boston. Despite the frigid temperature, they were suddenly on fire. The home-field advantage was evident as the Red Sox scored ten runs by the bottom of the second inning. I leaned up against the fence at the end of the bridge over the Mass Pike and made a mental list of the bills I needed to cover. I held the sign and an envelope of stickers in one hand, leaving my other free and ready to take cash and make change from the small apron tied around my waist. Single dollars would go in my left front pocket, fives in my right, tens and twenties in a third pocket in the back of my jeans. I took a deep breath, looked ahead, and waited.

The sound of the Charles River–inspired song "Dirty Water" by the rock band the Standells, echoing from the speakers inside Fenway Park, signaled that the Sox had won as people began to exit. At first, there was a trickle of fans on the sidewalk leaving the stadium, soon followed by an enormous rush that overtook the streets around the park as they made their way into Kenmore Square. I stood in the center of the sidewalk, parting the crowd as they walked by, trying to make eye contact while holding the sign over my head with one hand and a few stickers in the other. People chuckled as they passed, pointing at the sign. Standing there reminded me of standing outside after gigs to hand out my punk-music newsletter as people left, but on steroids.

"Get your stickers he-ah!" I yelled, pronouncing *here* with as heavy of a Boston accent as I could muster, inspired by the ticket scalpers I'd heard as they shuffled around the stadium before games. The crowd thickened, so I stepped closer to the curb to be near the center of the masses who had moved into the street once the sidewalk had become overfilled. Buying a souvenir from a street vendor was part of the game-day experience, just like buying a printed program or a Fenway Frank hot dog, and I was in business.

But no one was buying. I felt like I was in one of those dreams where you're naked in public, completely exposed and filled with self-doubt. I had convinced myself this would be big, and I started sweating as people walked by without buying anything. It took a moment to get the first sale, but a guy in a Nomar Garciaparra jersey approached with a five-dollar bill.

"Give me three of those!" he said as he turned to his buddy with a big grin and told him, "Putting one of these on Joe's car. He's going to be so pissed," he said, sharing the purchase was a prank on a friend who was a huge Yankees fan. When those first people stopped, others started to line up behind them. No one seemed to want to approach a lone vendor, but folks got in line once someone else broke the ice.

One after another, I traded stickers for cash with excited fans. Two dollars each, or three for five dollars when I could get the upsell, which was most of the time. The pockets of my apron and jeans bulged as the transactions blended together. My friends were doing just as well selling shirts, as I observed a constant flow of people with white T-shirts in their hands pass by while I worked to keep up with the demand. We were ecstatic. After thirty minutes, the crowds thinned, the streets emptied, and it was clear that I had made my last sale. I tucked away my sign and apron in my backpack and walked back to Mission Hill as the other guys loaded their remaining shirts into boxes.

I looked around nervously. I wasn't sure how much money I now carried, but it was a lot more than the twenty dollars I'd scraped together as change before walking to Fenway Park. Muggings were common in the area, so I kept my head down, walked briskly, and stayed aware of my surroundings. Once I was safely back inside my apartment bedroom, I started pulling the cash out. I straightened the money and arranged them in fifty-dollar piles.

One hundred. One-fifty. Two hundred. Two-fifty. Three hundred. Three-fifty. A few extra random fives and singles brought the night's earnings to $384. I looked at it all in disbelief. I'd made more money in a few hours than I had all week at my real job. It was more than I had earned doing anything in that short amount of time. This windfall was cold, hard cash, and I could do it again tomorrow night, and the next two nights after that! With eighty more home games at Fenway Park ahead of me this season, I could bankroll my record label by printing and selling the rivalry with the Yankees to Red Sox fans.

Within days, everyone involved in Fenway's street economy felt our presence. My friends and I descended on the crowds that left the stadium like locusts, and the 21-ers watched in frustration like horrified farmers as we devoured their livelihood and disrupted the market with no regard for anyone else. There hadn't been any pleasantries exchanged when we arrived; we just showed up and sold as much stuff as possible. I could feel them sizing us up as they stared. These guys had dominated the season before and were now watching as fan after fan bought from us instead. One night after selling had wrapped up, they finally approached.

The crowds had all left, and the lights above Fenway Park had gone dark. Worm and Rod were boxing up their remaining shirts, and the rest of us were chatting when three of the 21-ers walked up to us. One of them approached Rod and asked, "Hey, where are you guys from?"

"Who wants to know?" Rod replied as he tucked in the cardboard-box flap to close it.

"We've been selling shirts here for a while and hadn't seen you guys before. Are you working for Sal?" the 21-er continued.

"Sal who?" Rod responded.

The 21-er made a slight grimace. "If you don't know Sal, you probably shouldn't be out here."

He tried to say it with authority, but his voice had a trepidation to it. Was he implying we needed permission to be on the sidewalk in the middle of the bridge?

"Yeah? Well, fuck you, and fuck Sal," Rod replied, after assessing the threat and motioning at us. "I've got eight guys; *you* get the fuck off this bridge." They stared at him, unsure what to do next, and opted to back down. These guys were inexperienced, and Rod had called their bluff. The 21-ers didn't try to tell us what to do after that.

We continued to spread out around Fenway Park, an opportunity unique to the stadium. It was the earliest Major League Baseball (MLB) park in use at eighty-eight years old, opening just five days after the *Titanic* sank in April 1912. Most teams by now had built modern venues on the outskirts of cities, with large parking lots that kept fans on private property and out of reach of independent vendors like us. But city streets surround Fenway Park in a congested Boston neighborhood. I stood on the sidewalk making sale after sale, while the other guys laid their shirts across the hoods of cars and hung them from chain-link fences surrounding the park.

The 21-ers' stock dropped, and to compete they had to lower the price of their shirts from twenty dollars to ten. Their profit margin shrank, and they couldn't offer the same commissions to their sellers as before. As a result, their crew got smaller, while ours continued to grow. Ironically, it turned out the 21-ers were a bunch of Northeastern student-athletes who weren't willing to fight for their hustle, punked by a Northeastern engineering student and his friends who would. And Sal? He wasn't a shadowy underworld figure, just a longtime vendor who sold photographs of Red Sox players. Sal leaned his framed pictures against a chain-link fence along the sidewalk and had likely been hawking on the street for a decade before the 21-ers arrived. We could handle the competition but learned we needed to contend with an actual threat: the Boston code-enforcement police.

As it turned out, you can't just walk up and start selling things out of a backpack in the streets of Boston—and if you do, the Boston code-enforcement police will be looking for you. Despite their badges and official-looking uniforms, code-enforcement officers were just about one tier above handing out parking tickets. They were employed by the city during the day and earned overtime working a paid detail for the Red Sox during games. Tasked with enforcing codes pertaining to illegal dumping and unshoveled sidewalks, one of their responsibilities was to also police unpermitted street vending, putting their attention squarely on us. They circled the stadium in little city-issued patrol cars with flashing yellow lights, carrying thick citation books. A single unauthorized sale by a vendor netted a $200 fine—*if* they caught you. They had a pretty cushy gig, for the most part. Mainly, it seemed to involve sitting in their cars and listening to the game on the radio. We referred to them as Codees.

The officer in charge of the Codees was a heavy-set townie who went by the nickname Tiger. He was just a few years older than the rest of us and, as a native of the working-class neighborhood of Dorchester, had a thick Boston accent. While only in his late twenties, he was on track to becoming a career city employee. At first, Tiger and the rest of the Codees didn't appear to be a regular fixture at the park; I'd see them only every few games.

To avoid them, I learned to calculate the ideal setup time: too early, and we were sitting ducks on the sidewalk while they quickly drove around the park, but if our crew came out as the game ended, the streets would become so clogged with people that their cars could no longer navigate. We were in the clear unless the Codees ventured out of their vehicles, which they rarely seemed to do. That timing was the difference between being chased away from the park with nothing to show for it or walking back to Mission Hill with our pockets swollen with cash. But, either way, there was another game the next night or a series the following week.

On a Saturday afternoon that May, as I stood on the bridge over the Mass Pike, the Red Sox had just begun a series against the Tampa Bay Devil

Rays. My lower back was damp with sweat, the downside of having something strapped over my shoulders when the temperature pushed eighty degrees. The Sox lost the game, with the Rays scoring the only run in the eighth inning. The crowd was disappointed, despite having watched starting pitcher Pedro Martínez get seventeen strikeouts, tying his career-high record. I held the sign advertising my goods high in the air as the street filled with people around me. Sales had been all right, but not great. Had the Sox won it would have been better, but I was still grabbing sales one after another. I'd just sold a three-pack of "Yankees Suck" stickers to a guy when I felt a pull from behind on my backpack, unbalancing me.

"I gotcha," I heard in a muffled Boston accent. It was Tiger. He had a firm grip on the nylon handle at the top of my bag. I'd already had close calls with Tiger, but this time he had me dead to rights. I held my sign and an envelope full of stickers; the only items in the bag were bundles of stickers that had probably cost me 30 bucks to make. I had to think quickly: old backpack and some cheap inventory, or a $200 fine? I relaxed my shoulders, sliding out of the straps, and immediately started running toward the bridge's other end. Tiger stood there dumbfounded, holding my backpack in the air in front of him. I quickly disappeared into the crowd.

Almost getting collared by Tiger convinced me we needed a more proactive plan to deal with the Codees. A quick exit was necessary when they walked up in their distinctive light-blue shirts and navy-blue pants. Rod and I took a trip to the Fenway Park neighborhood when the Red Sox were out of town to scope out potential escape routes. We ventured down every alley around the stadium to determine the best path out from our high-traffic selling spots. We walked past the rusted, leaky dumpsters and the garbage overflowing onto the broken asphalt, around the corner and out of sight from fans walking by on the sidewalk. Rod wore a backpack that carried the bolt cutters he used to crack padlocks that secured the mountain bikes he stole. It sliced through the many chain-link fences in the neighborhood with ease. He squeezed the handles tightly, clipping enough links until we could push the fence apart just enough to slip through.

I assigned each route a letter. For example, suppose the Codees saw you vending on Lansdowne Street. In that case, you chose Route C and could run down the driveway between the Cask 'n Flagon and a parking garage to a hole in the fence that led to the train tracks, allowing an escape south toward the Fenway commuter station. I distributed maps I'd printed on my desktop computer to hawkers with a satellite image of the Fenway neighborhood, highlighting the areas with the holes and alleys available for escape if we were unfortunate enough to be caught in the act. We were all relatively physically fit, while none of the Codees were winning a push-up contest anytime soon. And the bigger they were, the more aggressively they enforced the code. They might give chase, but there was no way they would catch us once we reached a fence, hole or no hole.

I started packing a hat and a brightly colored T-shirt in my backpack in case I needed to quickly change clothes and blend into a crowd when being pursued. We even went so far as to hire friends to follow the Codees and report back to us using two-way radios, ensuring constant updates on the area they patrolled around the park. This worked for a while until the Codees became hip to it and laughed while listening on their own radios to us calling in their coordinates as we tailed them around the park.

The gig beat working a regular job making $7.50 an hour, but the money didn't always come easy. One afternoon, one of my recruits, Matt, walked with Wes as his "lookout." While cutting through Kenmore Square, they crossed paths with Officer Tiger and another Codee looking for ticket scalpers. The Codees yelled for him to stop, and he tried to dart past one of them in between cars and got tackled. Tiger injured his thumb as he attempted to restrain Matt, so he told him, "We weren't going to arrest you; now we're going to take you in for assault and battery and resisting arrest!"

Wes called me to report what had happened, and Elisabeth had to go down to the station with the $500 in cash needed to bail Matt out. The charge for hawking without a permit during a restricted time—the very reason they stopped him—got dropped in court, but they stuck him with three hundred hours of community service for the "assault." The court would drop the charge if he stayed out of trouble for six months, so that was Matt's first and last time selling for me at Fenway.

Though the Codees and competing vendors were the two main hazards we faced, a third threat soon took us by surprise: our customers. Some of the biggest assholes I'd ever met came out of Fenway Park, and most of the physical violence that ensued resulted from drunk and disorderly Sox fans, tired of watching their team lose and looking for a fight as they exited the game. Fistfights were common early on, but they rarely happened with New York fans, as you might have expected. More often, they were with Boston fans who attempted to steal T-shirts out of vendor hands and carts as they walked by.

In the decades before our arrival, Red Sox fans sometimes took their frustration out on the "weird-looking" punk-music fans who hung out in Kenmore Square's longtime rock club, the Rathskeller. Colloquially known as the Rat, it was a dirty venue that had been a cultural fixture in the city since opening in 1974, comparable to the iconic CBGB club in New York City. The Rat's stage was Boston's introduction to rock and punk bands like the Ramones, Talking Heads, and the Cars; even the Police performed there in 1978. In the 1980s, the Rat became a popular place for hardcore-punk afternoon matinees, so concertgoers would hang out on the sidewalk in front, about a block from the entrance to the Kenmore subway station, where Red Sox fans passed by before and after games. This proximity led to the occasional altercation between Sox fans and punks, usually instigated over the counterculture appearance of the Rat's patrons.

The Rat had closed its doors a few years before we started hawking shirts and stickers. The neighborhood was turning over and getting nicer, so there was no longer room for a grimy punk club, and the building it was in was scheduled for demolition to make way for the 245-room Hotel Commonwealth. Despite losing the iconic club, Boston's hardcore punks still congregated in Kenmore Square. Instead of seeing a band perform in a venue that had infamously used kitty litter on the floors to mitigate flooding after a torrential rainstorm, we were waiting for the Red Sox game to finish so we could rake in as much money as possible. Sports fans still targeted us for our appearance, and we were deflecting the occasional expletives directed at us because of our hairstyles or tattoos, but we always had numbers. Friends who weren't selling for us came to the bridge over the Mass Pike to hang out, so there were always more of us than it appeared.

Provocation from Sox fans was becoming a regular occurrence. After yet another altercation one afternoon, out of frustration, I walked over to the little souvenir shop at the top of Lansdowne Street and dropped a hundred bucks on twenty of the eighteen-inch Red Sox mini baseball bats. "The next person who fucks with us, hit them with one of these," I said as I walked along the bridge and handed a bat to everyone standing there.

The following week, those bats were put to use. It was a warm afternoon after a Sox win against the Chicago White Sox, and six of us were working the bridge, trying to keep up with the demand. The "Sucks" guys pulled T-shirts out of boxes and tossed them over the shoulders of customers while I stood in front, pulling cash from the crowd and giving back handfuls of stickers. As each customer left, another took their place. In the swarm of people surrounding us on the sidewalk, two guys stood out as they approached.

We were used to people being loud as they left the game and often dealt with drunken fans. Plenty of obnoxious and intoxicated people had walked by without issue, and many of them had been great customers. But as I stuffed a five-dollar bill into my pocket, I could sense these guys were going to be trouble. Behind me, one of Worm's guys stood beside his cart, waving a T-shirt in front of himself to get attention. As the guys passed him, one grabbed a shirt draped over the edge of the cart behind the vendor's back. Different sizes of each tee had been positioned for easy access to the vendor, but that made them easy for people walking by to grab too. If the vendors weren't paying attention, they would *literally* lose their shirt.

"Hey!" I shouted to the vendor and pointed at the guy. "That dude just stole your shit!" The shirt hung from his hand as he walked away, unaware we were hip to the theft. I ran over and tried to grab the shirt as it swung by his side, but the guy held on; he wasn't giving it back.

Jesse Standhard, who was sitting on the railing against the chain-link fence behind the vendor, slid down and walked up to the guy. Jesse was used to swinging a bass guitar or microphone onstage, but that day, as the thief turned around to face me, Jesse swung the mini bat at the guy's head, splitting open his closely shaven scalp. Standing next to Jesse, Wes began hitting the guy's friend. I grabbed the first guy, and we exchanged a few punches. His shirt was mostly torn off in the ensuing struggle. I felt the knuckles of his fist impact my jaw, knocking my teeth together and chipping my lower incisor, enough so that every dentist I've seen since has asked if I wanted it fixed.

Everyone scattered, and selling was finished for the day. We met back up on Mission Hill; Jesse and Wes still had the guy's blood on their hands. My own shirt—a favorite from Ten Yard Fight's final tour—was stretched out and ripped at the collar. We were a little too eager to give chase and fight to retrieve stolen merchandise. Still, the flow of blood stopped the flow of cash, and we quickly learned that fighting cost us money and brought unnecessary heat down on us from the stadium and police. It wasn't worth risking an assault charge or getting shut down over a ten-dollar T-shirt that cost only two bucks to make.

Despite these regular hassles with the drunk and disorderly, the response from most fans around Fenway Park was overwhelmingly positive. They loved the sentiment on our merch and couldn't get enough; I was selling out of all the stickers and buttons I'd brought night after night. In the first few weeks, we caused quite a stir, upsetting whatever delicate balance had been struck before we'd arrived. We were collectively competing against the 21-ers, but we'd also angered the souvenir stores by selling too close to their entrances. Our crew offered something every fan wanted that wasn't available in their expensive and Major League Baseball–licensed brick-and-mortar shops, and the volume of our rent-free sales upset them. A proprietor on Brookline Avenue at the top of Lansdowne Street was so enraged he came out of his store one afternoon and threatened a street vendor with the long metal hook used to pull the security grate down in front of his shop. He swung it over his head as he yelled, "Get the fuck away from my store!" Pressure from the souvenir stores turned into calls to the police, prompting the city's code-enforcement details to descend upon us. The $200 fines and hassles over impounded products became an additional cost of doing business.

I wasn't the first street peddler with aspirations of becoming a CEO who had come to Fenway Park. There was precedent, most notably with Twins Enterprises, the owners of the souvenir shops that took issue with us selling too closely. More than fifty years earlier, that company had gotten their start in the same manner—by hawking products in the streets around the stadium. Twin brothers Arthur and Henry D'Angelo began what would become Twins Enterprises by selling souvenirs and scalping tickets to Red Sox fans, racking up some serious cash—as well as a few arrests—in the process. Over the years, their hustle helped them build Twins into a heavy hitter in the sports-licensing world. The brand that they started (these days known as '47) is now owned by New Era and does hundreds of millions of dollars in sales each year. I was doing thousands of dollars in sales—which to me felt like millions—and their story was an inspiration if ever there was one. It was also proof that what I had started might someday grow larger than I could ever imagine—*if* I kept hustling.

The span of the bridge where we most often sold became valuable territory. Soon our success inspired other hopeful entrepreneurs, which presented a problem. We had limited space to work, and every time someone new entered the square, each slice of the pie got a little smaller. And if a newbie's presence meant we went home with less money, that wasn't going to fly. The 21-ers had failed to contain us, and when others arrived and tried to sell nearby, we used our collective numbers to persuade them to move deeper into Kenmore Square, farther away from the stadium. We'd get first dibs on fans leaving Fenway.

We felt we'd earned it for ourselves, after all of our confrontations with code enforcement and the losses we'd taken up to that point. Newcomers weren't privy to any of that; they just saw the empty stretch in front of us as an open opportunity, not realizing it wasn't up for grabs. Street rules applied: we didn't abide by typical business pleasantries. It was important to send a clear message quickly, especially if telling them to beat it didn't work. Occasionally, we had to resort to low-level intimidation tactics. We weren't professional knee-breakers. We just wanted to nudge people out of the way because a lot of money was at stake.

One evening as we were selling, I noticed white T-shirts in fans' hands as they walked by. This was alarming because no one should have been selling in front of us. One held a shirt up to a friend to show off what they'd just bought, and the collegiate lettering on the front looked familiar.

"Hey, man, what do you have there?" I asked the guy as he strolled past.

"A 'Yankees Suck' shirt," he replied, holding it against his chest.

I glanced at the tee. It looked like someone had called a screen printer and described Worm's tee, and what they came up with had the same vibe. It had navy-blue ink on a white shirt, and "Yankees Suck!" in a hollow, outlined font with an exclamation point, centered across the shirt's chest. It was a watered-down version of Worm's wares.

"Where'd you get it?" I inquired.

"In front of the Cask. Some guys were selling them out of a box," he said, as he pointed toward the bridge behind him, referencing the Cask 'n Flagon restaurant.

I motioned to R.J., one of Worm's vendors standing close by. "Someone's cutting us off," I explained. "Let's go check it out."

We walked through the swarm of fans leaving the game. As we got closer to the stadium, we could see two guys standing, facing the crowds, one of them holding a white shirt in the air. I walked up alongside the guys and asked, "What the fuck do you guys think you're doing?"

The guy holding the shirt looked over at me. He had a thin chin-strap beard and a backward Sox hat, a cigarette tucked behind his right ear. He was probably from Melrose, Malden, or maybe Medford. He likely took the Orange Line train into the city with his buddy to sell shirts and earn some beer money.

"We're selling shirts, khed," he replied, pronouncing *kid* with a distinctive Boston accent.

"This spot is spoken for; you're going to have to leave," I said.

He looked around, not seeing anyone else selling nearby. "It's a free country," he replied.

Ah, the "free country" response. I looked at the guy and said, "Oh? Got it." *Let's see how this shakes out*, I thought.

R. J. and I glanced at each other and nodded. We couldn't let these guys get a taste of the money and needed to motivate them to walk a few hundred feet behind us or leave and never return. If they knew how good it was, we'd never get rid of them—they'd get addicted just as we had. Get them to bounce now, and they wouldn't know what they're missing. When confronted, most followed the path of least resistance; they would pack up their shirts and either go to the end of the line or give up completely. When someone pushed back, we had to get creative.

As we walked back to the rest of our crew in Kenmore Square, R. J. continued to the 7-Eleven. I pulled aside Worm and a few of the guys hanging around. Minutes later, R. J. returned, a sixty-four-ounce bottle of grape juice in each hand. These new guys were about to learn that being in a free country wouldn't stop someone else from turning their T-shirts purple.

Our beef with guys like this wasn't strictly over competition. That was part of it, but mainly it was because they were knocking off our product. You might ask, how is what they did different from what Worm had done? The way I saw it, Worm had taken something that already existed and made it better, appealing to a larger audience. These guys? They had taken what Worm was doing and somehow made it shittier.

Six of us walked back over the bridge toward the two guys. R. J. handed one of the bottles to Jamey, who unscrewed the top as we approached. Worm shouted at the guys, his frantic energy taking them by surprise. R. J. stood next to Worm in front of the guys while Jamey approached from behind, and they both began pouring the grape juice all over the open box of shirts, instantly turning the white cotton a shade of violet.

"Aww, what the fuck!" the backward-hat vendor exclaimed, putting his hands on his head as he watched his inventory get rendered worthless. His friend lowered the shirt he had been holding up, and his eyes darted at each of us. These guys were outnumbered and not in a position to do anything about it. Once it was clear their shirts were ruined, we started to walk away. Worm kicked the box on the ground between them, knocking it over and spilling the stained shirts onto the sidewalk. We didn't see those guys again.

I was paying fifteen cents for a bumper sticker and a quarter for a button while selling them at a 1,900 percent markup and getting a massive return for my efforts. We were profiting like drug dealers without the risk. Most of the crew earned a couple of hundred dollars per game, just hawking merch and hanging out with their friends. I recruited two friends and gave them signs and courier bags full of stickers. They sold my swag and earned a 30 percent commission, helping me pocket thousands of dollars every home stand.

CHAPTER 8

The Sketchy Lot

BACK AT MY APARTMENT EVERY NIGHT AFTER LEAVING FENWAY Park, I bundled hundred-dollar stacks faster than I could spend them, channeling all my cash into releasing American Nightmare's record and sparing no expense. The money had already helped pay for most of their recording, but I still needed to cover that last studio bill. I also needed to make promotional posters and postcards and place ads in magazines. Meanwhile, Worm and Rod's crew celebrated every dollar, dropping their newfound gains on expensive watches, thick silver chain necklaces, overseas travel, and dinners at five-star restaurants. They lived largely and began referring to themselves as International Men of Leisure.

The fast money combined with being young and easily entertained were how I found myself in the dimly lit Sketchy Lot after midnight on a deserted stretch of Mission Hill, about to fight a friend. A dozen spectators, their pockets packed with cash, waited to see a bare-knuckle fistfight. Davey, shirtless and loosening his arms, paced back and forth. We began to circle each other, keeping our fists up, but neither making a first move. It felt awkward just jumping right into it, so I made a couple of punching motions as if I was getting warmed up, and the first few swings were almost playful, just punching the air. There was a part of me that wondered if we would both commit to it. I had no issues with Davey, but the desire to add what I hoped would be a quick five hundred dollars to my growing indie-label war chest motivated me to approach him and take the first real swing.

With a loud smack I connected with Davey's temple, and there was no turning back.

Davey fell back and slid onto the sandy asphalt before rushing over with both fists flying. It was on. We exchanged a flurry of punches, one after another. I came at him and landed another on his face, then a punch with my left fist to his nose. I quickly tried to backhand him with my right fist but lost my balance and started falling backward as he threw several more punches that got caught up in my arms as I swung them in front of me. I righted myself and started leaning forward as I walked toward him. Davey's nose had begun to bleed. As he put his hand up to wipe away the dripping blood, I paused to ask, "Are you all right, dude?"

"Yeah," Davey replied, wiping the blood on his jeans.

"Cool," I said, ready to continue.

The group laughed, clearly not expecting a moment of civility during a parking-lot winner-takes-all fistfight.

We exchanged several blows, and I did what I could to end the fight despite my growing exhaustion. I landed another jab to his nose with my left fist.

"Remember," Rod announced, "you guys decide when the fight's over: whoever submits."

I threw another punch and completely missed. Davey took the opportunity to rush at me, but I quickly righted myself. My next punch connected with a thud, Davey's slight wince signaling the fight had tipped in my favor. He reached up and held his face before turning around to try to run a few paces away to give himself a moment to recover. I ran alongside him, reached out, and grabbed him around the neck, using his momentum to push him to the ground onto his back. I pinned him down with my knee and began punching him repeatedly in the face with my right fist, hoping he would soon submit so this could be over. After the third punch connected, Davey started shouting, "Fuck, fuck! Stop, stop!"

"Are you done?" I asked as I pinned his wrists to the pavement above his head.

"Yes," Davey replied as Rusty started saying, "That's it, that's it," calling the fight.

Everyone started clapping. I stood, relieved it was over, and helped pull Davey up. We shook hands as the group surrounded us, high-fiving and congratulating us.

"Oh my god, are you all right, man?" Rusty asked Davey.

"Yeah," Davey replied, leaning over to catch his breath.

Rod walked up to Davey and gave him a little push from behind.

"That was an amazing fucking fight, dude," he said, pointing at him. Davey deserved most of the credit for blindly agreeing to fight in the first place without knowing whom his opponent would be. I had a newfound respect for him and knew everyone else did after they saw him step up like that. I walked back up to Davey, who still had his hands on his knees, breathing heavily, and shook his hand again.

"C'mon, pay up!" Rod announced, taking a handful of twenty-dollar bills out of his pocket and holding it up. "You guys just had the best fucking show."

Everyone pulled the cash they'd earned that week selling "Yankees Suck" merch out of their pockets and passed it to Rod. He turned to me smiling, satisfied with the evening's entertainment, and handed me the prize money. I peeled a hundred dollars off the top and gave it to Davey; he deserved something for his efforts. As the crowd dispersed back to whichever apartments they'd been hanging out at, I folded the bills, slid them into my pocket, and said my goodbyes as I walked up Hillside Avenue back to bed.

The lights were still on, so I opened the door and entered the bedroom, where Elisabeth anxiously awaited my return. To her surprise, I tossed the thick wad of cash on top of her comforter. As I recounted what had just gone down, I looked at my face in her mirror, assessing any potential damage. There was no blood or bruising, but my knuckles were sore and starting to swell. I slowly opened and closed my right hand to ensure I had movement in each finger. Relieved but not necessarily impressed, Elisabeth walked into the kitchen, bringing back a bag of frozen peas for my hand.

"Sorry I kept you up," I said as I turned off the light and returned to bed. Elisabeth would be headed to her office job in just a few hours, and my friends' late-night boredom, penchant for high jinks, and ambition (or lack thereof) had interrupted her sleep. Jumping at an opportunity that had served me well in my past had paid off yet again, and I smiled to myself as I drifted off to sleep, four hundred dollars closer to releasing American Nightmare's record.

CHAPTER 9

On the Map

THE RED SOX WERE TIED WITH THE YANKEES TEN WEEKS INTO the 2000 season, with thirty-five wins and twenty-nine losses. New York had just been swept by the Chicago White Sox, giving up forty-two runs while scoring only seventeen times during a four-game series. Boston fans smelled blood in the water and hoped to get ahead of the Yankees. When the Red Sox and Yankees met up for their third series in mid-June, Yankee catcher Jorge Posada blasted the ball into the center-field bleachers and put three runs on the Green Monster scoreboard for New York. Shortstop Derek Jeter's home run in the fourth inning added two more. The Red Sox got one run in during the seventh but gave up a mind-numbing sixteen runs between the final two innings, getting crushed 22–1, a new low.

I rode my skateboard to the Mission Hill post office in the morning, a trip that became a weekly errand. I had a handful of packages to ship out, but I was there mainly to purchase a money order to make the final payment on the American Nightmare recording. I took the cash I'd pocketed after the fight and laid the stack of twenties before me. I added a hundred bucks and some change to cover the rest, some of it money I'd earned earlier in the week after a Sox game, and wrote the studio's name on the "pay to the order of" line. Tearing the receipt off at the perforated edge, I slid it into a stamped envelope and placed it on the counter.

Little green money-order receipts like that one piled up on my desk at my apartment as I mailed the payments to the many vendors with whom I was racking up bills. Advertisements in fanzines, promotional materials, office supplies—anything I thought I might need to help push the label and, more important, American Nightmare.

The band's self-titled record finally landed on store shelves in July 2000. Each record was individually folded and sealed with a hand-glued strap of printed card stock that featured the band's name, a distinctive design element that gave it a unique look. Still, I could have strangled the graphic artist, Jacob Bannon, for this design because it was a pain in the ass to execute, as every cover had to be hand-assembled, one at a time, by me. Late one night leading to the EP's release, I found myself up at two in the morning with dried glue all over my fingers as I tried to affix the straps around each record cover. Albums were laid out to dry on every flat surface surrounding me. The printed band around the record was a nice touch, but it had added twenty hours of assembly time, and I was exhausted and lightheaded from the glue and lack of sleep. I didn't know it then, but these extra details soon proved to be more than worth it. Not only were American Nightmare and their self-titled 7-inch unique in their own right, but it was also a record that would go on to put the band, and Bridge Nine, on the map, as it was soon met with universal acclaim.

American Nightmare supported the record with an intense live performance, playing out often on the road. I accompanied the band to their first twenty shows, bouncing around the East Coast and into Canada in their rented minivan, including a stint that found me on driving duty and trying to hit 120 miles per hour on the highway as we approached Montreal. They played out-of-the-way venues and regularly returned to Maine, where they gathered a dedicated following.

Wes became a strikingly compelling front man with a penchant for symbolic self-deprecation, frequently wrapping his microphone cord around his neck like a noose. His lyrics had a melancholy tone but drew fans to them in a way that I had not yet seen with one of my bands. In American Nightmare's songs, Wes sang his personal reflections with a balance of sadness and anger that resonated with a legion of fans struggling through their own shit. It was clear to me that Wes was meant to do this. His thoughts had been bottled up in journals, notebooks, and inside himself, and now they were free.

American Nightmare didn't have to fight to find an initial fan base: a small one was ready and waiting, and it multiplied. The band built a following primarily because of the chaos that started onstage and the energy that flowed into the audience, which grew larger at every show, and word spread about how powerful they were. Wes's intensity was undeniable, and, soon, the entire crowd shouted each word of every song along with him. The band represented a changing of the guard in the Boston punk-music scene, and while they quickly recruited new fans, they struggled to move some current gatekeepers who felt that the band's early gains were undeserved. The hype and anticipation for American Nightmare were a recipe for jealousy and questions as to why they were getting interest when band X, Y, or Z wasn't. The hardcore-punk subculture is no different from the rest of the world regarding opportunities: it's all about who you know. People open doors for their friends first, myself included. But this band was going somewhere, and there wasn't anything anyone could do to stop them. There was something special happening, and if a door *didn't* open, they were going to kick it down themselves. Having moved a few thousand copies, their new EP became Bridge Nine's best-selling release. As far as the pop-music charts were concerned, it wasn't a significant accomplishment, but the band was earning a well-deserved buzz, the label was growing, and people were starting to notice.

CHAPTER 10

The Bouncer

IN THE SUMMER OF 2000 I WASN'T EARNING AS MUCH AS MY T-shirt-hawking roommate, Rod, but I was making enough to get by while investing most of the money into my label and squirreling away the rest. What I walked home with after each game kept growing, from pulling in more than $500 to $800, a significant jump from the 250 bucks a week I had been making at Tower Records only months earlier to always having $1,000 in my pocket, just in case I needed it. As loud as the baseball fans were in the bleachers, they became my silent partner, people I could depend on for desperately needed funding. The neighborhood around Fenway Park was like one of those arcade-style money chambers, where cash flies inside a big glass box, and some lucky contestant needs to try to catch it as it flutters past like they're in the middle of a tornado. We grabbed whatever we could as soon as the games ended.

I graduated from hiding tightly packed envelopes of bills in the back of a dresser drawer to filling a heavy safe at the bottom of my closet with $1,000 bundles. It wasn't long before we all had safes in our Mission Hill apartments to secure the money we were making. Word began to spread about how all of the Mission Hill punks were cashing in at Fenway Park, and it wasn't long before I heard from one particular individual who wanted to know more.

Over the years, the Boston hardcore-punk music scene had earned a reputation for being aggressive. There was a physicality that had developed as part of the culture, an undertone also found in other metropolitan areas where punk music and ideas had taken root. Within the scene, there were many characters you quickly learned not to cross, but I can say for certain that this individual was one of the most intimidating I'd met. He worked security details at a bar on Lansdowne Street and had played in local bands for more than a decade. A punk-rock Tyler Durden (the character played by Brad Pitt in the movie *Fight Club*), he was respected, if not feared, by many, as the stories of him and his crew of friends were passed along to the uninitiated by seasoned members of Boston's hardcore-punk scene. When I saw him during games, he was standing out on the sidewalk greeting nightclub patrons, but he wasn't some low-level door guy. He had curated a tightly knit network with two generations of the fiercest individuals within the hardcore-punk scene who'd fight alongside him at a moment's notice. Not someone to be fucked around with, he pulled many strings from behind the scenes. He was tough, but he was also an artist and an aspiring filmmaker. I'll refer to him here as the Bouncer.

Through the scene, we were acquaintances, and I'd go out of my way to say hello when I was on Lansdowne Street. He stood imposingly by the door of one of the clubs, checking IDs and wrapping colored paper bracelets around the wrists of drinking-age patrons as they entered. One of his most prominent features were his piercing dark eyes; you couldn't see beyond them. His handshake was firm, and he was well spoken. Despite always appearing guarded and serious, he had an energy and a laugh that helped cut the tension around him. I enjoyed talking with him and was thankful I had earned what seemed to be a rare spot in his good graces.

The neighborhood around Fenway wasn't just where my friends and I went to make money; for the past year, we had ended up along the stretch of Lansdowne Street where the Bouncer worked late on many Friday and Saturday nights, where'd we'd witness what we referred to as "the Two O'Clock Shuffle." That was the moment at 2:00 a.m. when the bright lights turned on inside the closing bars and clubs, and everyone was pushed outside.

This parade leaving the clubs was prime late-night people-watching entertainment highlighted by scantily clad clubgoers and highly intoxicated bros. While most of us were stone-cold sober, we would offer a play-by-play narration as we witnessed at least one alcohol-fueled fistfight or lover's spat per outing. We often hung back and watched it unfold, but I couldn't help but put ourselves into some of the action. One night I brought four sets of laminated cards with large, black single-digit numbers on them, so we could line up behind people with low scores held over our heads, rating unsuspecting clubgoers as if they were on a game show. None of the women scored above a four, no matter how attractive they were. The guys accompanying them never saw the humor in it, so I'm not sure how we got away with it without a fight breaking out.

Another night we watched an altercation start between two people in the middle of the street. Words escalated to fists as one person pushed another onto the hood of a car. Friends of each guy became entangled, as the driver and passengers involved themselves in the free-for-all. What likely started as shit-talking between strangers turned into a brawl involving at least a dozen people, much to my friends' delight as we leaned against the rail along the sidewalk, taking in the show. We didn't see it as real-world violence; it was like watching an Ultimate Fighting Championship bout on TV. It was a dependable—and, more important, free—form of late-night entertainment for people who, before the "Yankees Suck" hustle, could barely afford cable television, even when splitting the bill among roommates.

One evening as I walked past the Bouncer's bar, I stopped to say hello. After chatting about bands and music for a bit, he segued the conversation to asking about how sales had been going at Fenway, with specific questions as to how Worm and I operated. He'd had a front-row seat as we both hawked our products around the stadium during and after games and was curious if we were working together. I could feel the hair stand up on the back of my neck, and his questions were immediately concerning. I explained that we operated separately and described how Worm and I went about our own businesses. While independent from each other, we worked to reinforce the perception that we were all one crew to project an image of strength in numbers as a deterrent to potential competitors. If you had a problem with one of us, you had a problem with us all. Many vendors were friends and roommates, and several were playing in bands releasing records on Bridge Nine. We weren't hiring random people off the street; everyone was a friend of a friend because it was a cash business, and we needed to trust the people working for us.

"Good. If he's not working with you, I'm taking his stake," the Bouncer replied after learning the nuances of our arrangement.

Fuck, I thought as I looked back at him. I had to handle this delicately. I couldn't tell him what to do, but I didn't want to see Worm's operation usurped by the Bouncer. Rod and other friends involved with Worm's crew would also be affected, and it would likely just be a matter of time before my ability to earn there became compromised as well.

The Bouncer did not respect Worm, and his interest in the shirt hustle wasn't strictly business; it was also personal. He had recently begun dating Worm's ex-girlfriend, and her accounts of Worm having been physically aggressive with her had earned Worm a target on his back. The black eye she had a few months back? It wasn't from getting mugged on her walk home in Mission Hill, as she had told friends. Worm had given it to her during an argument. And the Bouncer had already beaten him up over it at least once.

Worm stood to lose a lot more if his shirt-slinging hustle at Fenway was targeted like the neo-Nazi punks who tried to infiltrate Boston's music scene years before had been. They were run out of Boston by the Bouncer and his friends through extreme violence, a purging that had become local lore. If Worm received the same attention from the Bouncer, it would be game over for his souvenir T-shirt business.

The Bouncer was curious how that would affect me, a courtesy I did not expect. Instead of taking over Worm's hustle, he ultimately chose to shake him down for a hundred dollars per game for "protection," which became an additional cost of doing business for Worm during those highly profitable early years. Worm's crew had sold more than a thousand T-shirts in a single afternoon, so paying a hundred bucks per game to avoid trouble seemed like a smart business decision. That leverage netted the Bouncer thousands of dollars throughout the Red Sox season, money he invested in an independent film he was producing, while letting Worm and Rod stay in control of their affairs at Fenway. In the end, Worm held on to his shirt hustle, but he had no idea how close he'd come to losing it all.

CHAPTER 11

Us Against Them

WHENEVER THE RED SOX WERE ON THE ROAD, I SCHEMED TO create new products and make even more money. I introduced new sticker designs, ensuring I would have enough options so that everyone took advantage of the three-for-five deal. Worm and Rod added to their shirt line with "Clemens Sucks," "Jeter Sucks," and others, taking shots at marquee Yankees players, and they started referring to themselves as "the Sucks Guys," which was later shortened to the Suckers. The culture of negativity we were curating around Fenway Park looked more like what Yankee Stadium had in the late '70s—and Red Sox fans were eating it up.

With our crew overrunning every exit around the stadium, coupled with the crude slogans we promoted, we invited more calls to the Codees. I knew there had to be some way to get them off our back and started asking questions. The Codees were there only to enforce the statutes and wouldn't offer help navigating them, so I learned from a hot-dog vendor that a license was available that could offer us a bit of reprieve. Massachusetts has what is known as a hawker-and-peddler permit. It only costs sixty-two dollars for an entire year, available the same day you apply, and is good statewide, though each city decides how it can be used. In Boston, it came with some tight restrictions, particularly that from 8:00 a.m. until 8:00 p.m., the permit was not valid throughout most of the downtown area. In addition, the permit was designed more for door-to-door selling and not meant for vending in one spot. That was reserved for a stationary-vending license, something no longer issued near Fenway. A handful of stationary-vending permit holders were grandfathered in and peppered around the stadium, but those had resulted from a negotiation between the city and vendors at the direction of Boston's city council years before we had come on the scene. As the vendors around Fenway Park learned in the late 1970s, we had to move after every sale, or every five minutes, whichever came first.

In June, less than two months after we started vending, I obtained my first hawker-and-peddler permit. When I saw Rod later that day in the kitchen of our apartment, I held it out as he closed the refrigerator door.

"What's that?" he asked, eyeing the little rectangular card tucked inside a plastic sleeve with a clip attached at the top.

"*This*," I replied as I held it closer to him, "is what's going to keep us from getting fucked with by the Codees." Rod took the permit and inspected it. I continued, "We can keep selling, and the Codees can't do shit."

I explained how it worked and its limitations, and Rod and Worm got theirs the following week. Our friends each filed down to the police station at Roxbury Crossing to complete their background checks before going to Boston's Government Center to apply for their permits. Half of our headaches dealing with code enforcement evaporated overnight with this fairly simple process. Now that we had a legitimate state permit to sell our wares, they would have one less opportunity to target us—at least after 8:00 p.m.

Unable to stop us for unpermitted vending after evening games—their previous strategy—the officers began following us to enforce the hawker-and-peddler statute to the letter of the law, ensuring constant movement. They'd stare at their watches before telling us to pack up and move at least fifty feet after each sale. If they felt we were yelling too loudly, they threatened to fine us because of the noise, and they didn't seem impressed when I pointed out that a hawker, by definition, was "a person who offers goods for sale by shouting." We were also a block from an open-air stadium filled with almost forty thousand people cheering and booing after every play, so we were far from making the most noise in the neighborhood. We frustrated them because we did everything possible to circumvent their efforts. Typically, when someone with a badge approaches, most people comply. But having grown up as punks, on the other hand, we had a healthy disrespect for authority as part of our DNA. And who exactly were we hurting? The money had already left the park. By the time it reached us, it was up for grabs, and we would do whatever we could to get it, Codees be damned.

I tried to ration every dollar earned, but the other guys were itching to spend. It wasn't uncommon to have two exotic dancers in full-length coats and a six-foot-four security guard in a full Adidas tracksuit show up at the front door, after Worm called a friend, who in turn called another friend to make it happen. These women probably hit three or four private parties a night between late Thursday night and early Sunday morning. It cost a couple of hundred bucks to get them in the door and then all the singles you could spare over the next thirty minutes. The money, as you can imagine, went quickly.

Rod had built stadium seating by placing a couch on top of a wooden bunk bed frame, with another sofa below it and a few extra chairs squeezed in around it. Fifteen dudes were crammed into what was basically a mini theater, so this would be a profitable stop for the women. Dollar bills rained down, covering the hardwood floor and coffee table as they worked the room.

It wasn't just our apartment floor with cash scattered all over it. All I could think about was money; I felt like I was manifesting it into existence. I saw it everywhere I went. It was like driving a specific car model; suddenly, you notice it wherever you go.

One night as Wes, R. J., and I walked up Tremont Street from our apartment with another friend, Jason, I saw a dollar on the sidewalk in front of an apartment building. I smiled as I reached down to grab it, and the moment I touched the bill, muffled laughter erupted from the darkened first-floor windows. I looked up, making out the huddled shadows of people peering at us. I exchanged looks with my friends and glanced back at the money. Something was off. I realized it was a poo dollar, a tasteless prank where someone places a folded dollar bill with shit smeared inside and waits for someone to come along and put it in their pocket. It's not something you should do in front of your own place in this neighborhood. The sound of their laughter stung.

"They know that *we* know where they live, right?" I asked Wes, anger rising inside of me.

The prank might have been harmless, but I wasn't going to let us be their entertainment for the night. I stepped around the right side of the house into the alley between buildings, looking for something heavy. In the darkness, I tripped over a log-size piece of a tree trunk as thick as my thigh and roughly two feet long. Reaching down to pick it up with both hands, I appreciated its heavy weight and backed up to the sidewalk while balancing it over my right shoulder. I heaved the log into the air, shattering the window, the festive banter replaced by the sound of breaking glass. It was definitely overkill, but someone else could have done much worse in this neighborhood. The four of us immediately started running the half block up to St. Alphonsus Street, where Wes, R. J., and I took a right and ran toward Huntington Avenue, while Jason took a left and ran up the hill by himself. Which was fine; at about 120 pounds, Jason wouldn't be much help if this ended in a fight. We made it about three blocks when we started getting winded because none of us had been prepared for the run.

Looking back, we could see a half-dozen figures under the streetlights as they rounded the corner in pursuit. Outnumbered, we started to run again, digging through our pockets for anything we could use in self-defense. I pulled out my cell phone and called the one person I knew would stop whatever he was doing and be ready to fight. The phone rang, and Rod answered. "What's up?"

"Rod! Wes and I ran into some trouble," I said, somewhat breathlessly. "We're getting chased and could use some help."

"Where are you?"

"We're heading toward the garage on Huntington across from Mass Art. Bring whoever you can; we'll need numbers," I said before hanging up.

A small independent gas station with a convenience store was at the intersection of St. Alphonsus and Huntington Avenue. It was a dirty garage with rolling galvanized-steel security grilles over the windows, a relic of an older Boston. The front door was open, and several employees hung out inside.

To their surprise, we ran into the store, sizing up the space while trying to devise a plan. Strategically, at least by being inside behind the small open front door, only one of our pursuers at a time could enter to get to us. That would help us deal with the fact that we were outnumbered at least two to one. Wes picked up a large padlock from one of the window sills. I had a keychain Kubotan, a pencil-size tool of Japanese design used for self-defense in close quarters, which R. J. passed to me as we ran. We stood our ground as the people chasing us sprinted to the front of the gas station.

"You fucked up," the guy who stood in front exclaimed as he pointed at me.

"What are you going to do about it?" Wes responded. He then hit himself in the head with the padlock and glared at them. It was a show of intimidation, something I'd seen him do with a microphone onstage.

Two of them forced their way into the small retail space to confront us, and we moved forward to respond. Punches were immediately thrown by all, and the employees began shouting agitatedly for us to get out. Several of the junk-food retail displays got knocked over, and within thirty seconds of the commotion, the entire record scratched to a halt when R. J., our typically more quiet and reserved friend, brandished a knife and held it out at arm's length. The guys from the Tremont Street apartment were not ready to be a party to what could have come next. And honestly, neither were we; the entire episode resulted from a stupid prank that had dramatically escalated.

Two police cars screeched into the small front parking lot from both streets of the intersection, their red and blue lights reflecting on the windows. R. J. dropped the knife and kicked it across the floor, where it slid under a rack out of sight. One of the squad cars had been sitting around the corner from the apartment that now had a gaping hole framed by shards of window glass. The cops had heard the breaking glass and connected that to the 911 call from the garage. They directed us to sit on the ground against the front of the building, the three of us on one side of the door, the six of them on the other.

At that very moment, the gravity of the situation began to set in. I stared straight ahead as I sat and wondered how I had let myself respond the way I did. I could have brushed it off. Was this worth getting us all arrested over it? Either way, this was where we were now, and it was going to be a long night.

The "poo crew" positioned themselves as victims, saying we'd vandalized their home and describing how we'd smashed their window open while they minded their own business. The cops started by telling my friends and me that we were all headed to lockup for the night, but as they began to piece together what had happened, they suggested we pay for the damage right then and there to avoid arrest. As the negotiation continued, Rod and a handful of our mutual friends arrived, having left mid-dinner at an Italian restaurant nearby. They lined up along the sidewalk, and Rod intimidatingly paced back and forth. It dawned on the pranksters that there were many of us, and we knew where they lived. After some deliberation with the guys who'd given chase, the police finally suggested that we leave in one direction, while they head home in the other—if only so they could avoid what would have likely amounted to hours of paperwork. So we all somehow ended up leaving the scene without getting arrested that night. I was relieved that my having broken the window hadn't gotten us into more trouble.

The following weekend, everyone from 9 Sewall planned to meet up with friends on the hill. Rod had some people visiting from out of town, and they'd been up in his room drinking before we headed out. Walking up Tremont Street, I started telling our guests the story of the melee from the week before. As we walked past the apartment with a newly replaced (and, unwisely, wide-open) front window, we could see that no one was inside, yet all the lights were on. Sensing an opportunity to raise the stakes and put another check in the win column, Rod put his hands on the open windowsill and hopped up, pulling himself into it.

Rod had become comfortable entering strangers' apartments. Not in a breaking-and-entering sort of way—he often played a game called "Where's Rod's Beer?" and would wander into buildings where a college party was happening in search of free booze. He'd work his way to the kitchen under the guise of a random partygoer and then walk off with a case of whatever was sitting unattended on the counter. He didn't care whose it was; he just acted and dealt with the fallout if it came.

Weeks earlier in Allston, a spur-of-the-moment alcohol poaching led to an all-out brawl in the street in front of some unwitting college kid's apartment. Rod had grabbed a case of beer and was confronted on his way out. Undeterred, he left the apartment with his prize and some agitated guy in tow questioning him, likely the person who'd brought the beer in the first place. As Rod ignored him on his walk back to meet us on the street corner, the guy grabbed Rod's shoulder to stop him. Rod responded by turning around and punching him in the head, knocking him into a large storefront window. He fell to the ground, but his friends saw their buddy go down and got involved.

As it all started to unravel, I spotted a familiar face I knew from the scene walking up the sidewalk. It was Gibby, a Boston punk veteran who sang for the Trouble, a local favorite. We made eye contact, and he could see something was up.

"Hey, man, are you good?" Gibby asked as he approached.

"It's us," I said, motioning to my friends, "against them," pointing to the people from the party.

Without hesitation, he dug into the courier-style bag that he had on, pulled out a bottle, and proceeded to wind up and throw it at one of the guys from the party like he was a pitching prospect for the Red Sox. The skirmish lasted only a few minutes, and I saw Galle holding another guy in a headlock, but as soon as we heard sirens approaching in the distance, we all broke out and ran from the area. The next day's newspaper had a police report about a dozen students from the party having been arrested, while we all made it home that night safe and sound.

But in Mission Hill at this very moment, with Rod climbing into the window I'd smashed a week earlier, trouble again found us. Rod stood up inside the apartment's living room. Surveying the scene, he walked over to the giant tube television against the wall opposite the window. It wasn't one of the slim televisions of today hung on a wall, but an older heavy-as-fuck model housed in the middle of a large entertainment cabinet. Rod leaned in and grabbed the TV from both sides. Picking it up, he stepped back and turned toward another open window on the other side of the room. He rested the unit on the edge of the window before shoving it through the opening, where it crashed onto the sidewalk below, shattering the screen with an incredible noise. The wires and various cable and control boxes connected to the wall still held on, stretching out from the sidewalk back through the window. Like the modified amplifiers in the movie *This Is Spinal Tap*, Rod had just taken it up to eleven, much to the amusement of his guests. Having lived with him for the past year, there was very little he could do to surprise the rest of us.

Not hearing any movement stirring in the apartment, we sensed no need to rush and started walking up Pontiac Street, leaving the shattered television surrounded by broken glass and plastic bits on the sidewalk behind us. We passed the Sketchy Lot and went down the alleyway behind a little industrial building rumored to be storage for the Museum of Fine Arts. We then crossed over to St. Alphonsus Street and continued up Calumet Street. At the corner of Calumet and Oswald Streets, we came upon a gathering of people partying in their yard behind a waist-high fence. Rod was easygoing when sober, but when he drank, he didn't give a shit and would say or do anything. For those of us who didn't drink, what happened next was usually somewhere between hilarious and highly stressful.

He started mouthing off a little to a few of the people closest to the sidewalk. No one in our group had anything to gain from an altercation with this random party, but Rod had set the night's tone just a few blocks ago. We were heading to meet up with friends, and, like we often did with Rod, things got a little out of control. The guys from the party didn't respond well to Rod, and I could already see that one of them, with the brim of his hat lowered over his eyes, held a knife by his side.

"Hey, Rod, let's keep moving," I said.

I don't think Rod heard me, but if he did, I was ignored. He continued to talk smack in his inebriated state.

At that moment, another group had turned the corner toward us about a block away. The poo crew, having been upstairs and upon hearing the commotion of their television unceremoniously leaving through their window, had come outside to investigate. That brought them up the street, where they happened upon us as Rod continued to push buttons. Knowing what was about to happen, we stepped back toward the overflowing garbage cans on the sidewalk. Wes grabbed a discarded frying pan from the top of the pile and held it by his side. Significantly outnumbered, we all opted to scatter and run farther down Calumet Street, cutting in between houses and climbing over fences in the dark to escape. The only one of us who got punched that night was Galle, and luckily he wasn't injured.

A few days later, as I walked past the Our Lady of Perpetual Help Grammar School while heading home, I noticed a Jeep drive down St. Alphonsus Street. I made uncomfortably prolonged eye contact with the front passenger and glanced back as they slowed down and pulled over. I didn't recognize the vehicle or the person, so whatever they wanted probably wasn't good, and I felt my body tense. I continued walking while holding my skateboard more tightly by my side, looking back as someone jogged toward me with both hands up as a sign of surrender. He'd remembered me from the previous two weekends.

"Hey, we want this to end. We don't want it to go any further." He extended a hand toward me.

I shifted my skateboard, slowly reached forward, and shook his hand with my right, nodding in agreement. It was over. Doing crazy shit for the thrill of it was exciting in the moment and often made for a great story afterward, but we were flirting with terrible consequences, and honestly, it was turning us into assholes. Any one of us could have been arrested for five different reasons that week alone. Someone could have gotten stabbed in that gas-station fight, or at that front-yard party, or punched, only to hit their head on the sidewalk—an injury that for an unlucky few meant game over. We were acting like that guy in Vegas whom I watched die, celebrating the moment without a care in the world, unaware he was seconds away from being dead on the street below. I didn't want to be that guy. I was twenty-four, no longer a kid, but I was acting like there were no repercussions, affecting people I was close to. I didn't win any points with Elisabeth after she had to pick Tim and me up from some alley on the other side of Mission Hill because our friends had fucked with too many people at once. Around that time, my mom had jokingly told her, "I would have torn that page out of the book by now," regarding having me as a boyfriend. I couldn't have blamed Elisabeth if she did.

Rod, though, seemed to thrive on chaos. If anything, he was ready to take more significant risks. A few nights later when we were hanging out in the living room at 9 Sewall, he told me about a high-rolling gambler he had seen at one of the casinos during his frequent poker trips, a regular who flashed a lot of cash, enough that it caught Rod's attention. "This guy is an easy mark," he said. "We should rob him."

I just stared at him. *After the week we've just been through?*

He stared back, not cracking his trademark smile, waiting for my response. Was this a test? Or some kind of joke?

"Wait, you're fucking *serious*?" I replied.

"Yeah. He's always there on the same nights and throws money around like he's trying to give it away. We could hit him in the parking lot. Split the cash."

He was so casual and confident about it that I couldn't immediately respond.

I'd never been particularly averse to risks. If anything, Rod had known me to take a lot of them, which is probably why he felt he could ask me in the first place. I was down to run around playing cops and robbers with the Codees at Fenway because they carried ticket books instead of guns, and at worst, we were risking a $200 fine. But armed robbery outside a casino? That would earn us a five-year prison sentence. When I was seventeen, I'd spent a single night in a jail cell after I'd broken a window at home during an argument with my parents; that had been enough for me. I wanted the money, but I just wasn't willing to cross that line. I needed to change the path that I was headed on because, for the first time, I'd started to feel like I had something truly significant to lose. My relationship with Elisabeth. The label. The bands that trusted me and relied on me.

"No," I told Rod, "I'm not down to do that, and if you are, you're fucking crazy."

Rod nodded his head. "Yeah, but you already knew that," he replied, with his mischievous grin and a telling gleam in his eye. "But you're probably right." Despite his "alpha" status, I don't think Rod would have graduated to that level of criminal activity alone. He needed another person to help him keep raising the stakes, whether it was a crazy prank or something more serious like this. I'd like to believe my shutting it down kept us from making a terrible decision.

I loved Rod's energy and grab-life-by-the-balls attitude, but there was a limit to what I was willing to do, which had become glaringly apparent during that short conversation. I still wanted to be one of the guys and keep things interesting with my friends, but my main focus needed to be on the label. I was trying to build something legitimately and wasn't willing to risk it anymore.

CHAPTER 12

Collateral Damage

WEDNESDAY, OCTOBER 4, 2000. FOR MOST OF THE 2000 SEASON, the Red Sox played over .500 ball, meaning they'd won more games than they'd lost, ultimately finishing with a barely winning record of eighty-five wins and seventy-seven losses, second to the Yankees in the American League East division. Boston missed the opportunity for postseason play when the AL wild-card spot went to the Seattle Mariners, who had finished their season with a higher win record at ninety-one. Despite losing fifteen of their final eighteen games and all of their last seven, the Yankees beat the New York Mets and won the World Series in just five games, much to the irritation of Red Sox fans. The last game of the regular Red Sox season occurred on October 1 when they fell to the Tampa Bay Devil Rays. For the first time in six months, the window of opportunity had closed, and I needed to make due with whatever I'd managed to save that season.

Tim and I were hanging out in my room a few days later talking about American Nightmare's upcoming West Coast tour. The band's debut was selling well and was already in its second vinyl pressing. Still, it was only an EP, and at the time, shorter records were not getting the same kind of traction in stores that full-length albums did. If we wanted this record to reach a bigger audience, we'd have to add some songs and eventually rerelease it as a full album. I knew the band was destined for a more prominent label—one that wasn't run from a roommate's bedroom—and I was both happy for them and proud of my contribution to helping them get to that level. They'd already written a few new songs and wanted to return to the studio.

Tim agreed to release a second 7-inch with Bridge Nine, but to make that happen, he asked me to front the money the band needed to buy plane tickets to Los Angeles. It would be their first trip to the West Coast for a four-day weekend of shows. Flying a band of five people across the country is expensive, but thankfully I was still sitting on a lot of "Yankees Suck" money. The season may have ended early for the Red Sox, but it had been good for me, and I still had a safe full of cash to reinvest in the efforts of my friends.

It was getting late, just after midnight. Suddenly, Tim and I heard numerous people rush down the wooden stairs next to my bedroom door. It sounded like they were jumping down the stairwell, only making contact with the landing in the center of the flight before leaping down to the hallway in front of my room. We were used to people coming and going at all hours, but something didn't sound right. Startled by their hasty departure, Tim looked into the hallway to see what the commotion was. Briefly, he made eye contact with one of them as the front door to the apartment opened, and they ran outside, disappearing into the darkness of the neighborhood.

While I'd been funneling the cash I earned at Fenway into my record label and financing all the new albums I was working on, Rod had been exploring less legitimate opportunities with friends he'd met in Boston's nightclub scene. He was a charismatic antihero, someone everyone liked to be around. Rod could have been successful at anything, but he reveled in the illicit. He wanted to be an outlaw and make his own rules with the same passion that most people want to fit in with the status quo and be told what to do, even though they won't admit to it. Remember that scene in *The Outsiders* when Ponyboy asks Dallas what he wants to do and Dallas responds, "Nothing legal"? That was Rod.

Unbeknownst to the rest of his roommates, Rod had been investing *his* earnings into buying wholesale quantities of weed to grow his customer base. As Tim and I discussed American Nightmare downstairs, Rod and his club-going friend Barry were looking to graduate from selling ounces to pounds, which put three people from the neighborhood into his third-floor bedroom late in the evening.

I later learned the deal was supposed to be five pounds for $25,000. It quickly went south as the buyers pulled out duct tape and guns instead; this wasn't a transaction but a robbery, and they planned to leave with the money *and* the weed. Outnumbered, Rod and Barry were shoved to the floor, their wrists bound with tape. The three men, dressed in jeans and dark hoodies, held on to the promised stash. The one pointing the gun at Rod motioned to the large safe perched in the dormer-style window.

Rod was instructed to stand up and open the safe. He may have conceded the money for the deal, but Rod was not giving up the rest of the bounty reaped from hustling his share of shirts at Fenway throughout the season. Rod broke free from the duct tape binding his wrists and rushed forward as he reached for the gun. That's when it fired, sending a single bullet into Rod's left cheek. Three floors below, the sound of the gun going off didn't make it down to where we were sitting. Despite being shot in the face, he knocked the firearm out of the assailant's hand. The robbers turned and ran out of the room, but with Rod trailing behind, pressing a wad of paper towels against one of the wounds. Blood squirted from between his fingers with each heartbeat as he ran down the stairs. It left red streaks on the walls and floor on his way down from his bedroom to the sidewalk and onto the street. Seth was returning from work at that very moment and had pulled his car up next to the house to park just as

Rod came rushing down the front steps. As his attackers disappeared into the dark streets of the neighborhood, Rod opened the passenger door and jumped in the car, to Seth's surprise.

"Seth! Get me to the fucking hospital!" Rod urged. "I've been shot. Let's go!"

Seth hit the gas and drove the eight blocks to Brigham and Women's Hospital, and Rod was admitted into the emergency room in critical condition. Doctors later said that the timing of Seth's sudden arrival and the emergency room's proximity saved Rod's life. The bullet had entered close to his chin and miraculously passed alongside his jawbone. It only nicked his carotid artery, which had resulted in the significant loss of blood left on the floor of his bedroom and splattered along the concrete where he'd gotten into Seth's car, but it wasn't enough to put Rod down.

Someone had called 911, resulting in a flurry of first responders descending upon 9 Sewall; red and white emergency lights reflected off of every window on the block and drew the attention of all our neighbors, bringing them to their doors and porches. Having not heard the gunshot ourselves, we didn't fully grasp what had happened until Wes, Galle, and Barry came downstairs. Shaken and confused, we were interviewed by police officers as homicide detectives collected evidence. A crime-scene photographer documented the bloody walls and floors, the flash of their camera repeatedly lighting up the stairwell inside our apartment.

After the detectives questioned each of us, we all went to the hospital to check on Rod; the whole crew gathered in the waiting room for updates. It had already been a long night, and everyone needed to sleep, so I trekked across the hill to Elisabeth's apartment, where I knew I could crash. I entered the stairwell and knocked on the door, but it was probably close to four in the morning, so no one answered. I dialed her cell-phone number and could tell I'd awoken her.

"Hello?" Elisabeth asked groggily.

"Someone shot Rod," I replied. "We've all left our apartment, so I need a place to stay tonight."

"Where are you?" she asked, suddenly sounding more alert.

"Here, at your door," I responded, and a few moments later she let me in.

At Elisabeth's place, the weight of what had just happened—and, even more stressfully, what could have happened just a few blocks over—was setting in. The guy that Tim had stared at as he left our house—had he pulled the trigger? What if he had thought he'd killed Rod? What would have stopped him from getting rid of the witnesses, that is, *us*?

I always knew the neighborhood had the potential to be dangerous. I'd hear about muggings, and there was one afternoon when two guys pushed me off my skateboard as I cut through Roxbury Crossing to get to the Big Wheel headquarters in Dudley Square. I didn't stick around to find out if they were planning to rob or beat me up; I hopped back on my board, and with two pushes of my foot, I was gone. So while I was aware of the potential for violence in the neighborhood, I had never been directly affected by it—until now.

The number of murders in Boston that year had begun creeping back up and stood at thirty-nine, a 25 percent increase from the previous year. Rod could have easily been number forty, but he was thankfully still alive and expected to recover. The next day the local news briefly reported on Rod's shooting but dropped it from the press shortly after. The only mention of it in print was six weeks later in an edition of the *Mission Hill News*, a neighborhood newspaper with a circulation of just four thousand copies. In addition to detailing Rod's shooting, it also reported on the stabbing of another Northeastern University student during a confrontation between two groups leaving a Hillside Street party late on the night of October 22. Witnesses described the suspect as having brandished a knife once words escalated to a physical altercation, reportedly stating, "I've used this knife before. Who do you think you're messing with?" before stabbing the victim in the lower back.

The assault occurred on the same block as Elisabeth's apartment, and I watched the police from her second-floor window as they interviewed neighbors the following day. The alleged stabber was described as a white male with an olive complexion wearing an orange baseball cap, a white T-shirt, and baggy jeans. It happened only a couple of blocks from the near brawl we'd barely gotten ourselves out of just months before, and the suspect sounded a lot like the person I'd seen holding the knife while Rod was mouthing off. Was it the same guy? Had Rod and the rest of us narrowly escaped danger before the shooting? Luck or not, we had been tempting fate, and a crash was inevitable.

With Rod's attackers on the loose, 9 Sewall was no longer a viable place to live; we weren't sure if anyone was watching us and didn't want to stay there any longer. Despite the shooting, the landlord wouldn't budge on the lease, so we broke it, daring him to come after us. He did, filing a lawsuit against us in housing court for unpaid rent within one month of our moving out, adding additional stress to all of us. This effort was later dismissed after an attorney provided by Northeastern University became involved. A three-bedroom apartment next to Elisabeth opened, and Tim and I moved in.

The shooting at 9 Sewall fractured the group. Rod went home to upstate New York to heal. He returned to Boston the following season to resume work with the Suckers, a long, jagged scar running up the side of his neck. He wanted to pick up where things had left off with his roommates, but resentment over the danger he'd brought into our apartment lingered. He'd gotten himself shot in our house, and any of us could have been collateral damage. Rod remained a friend, but priorities had changed for many of us, and things weren't going back to how they had been before.

CHAPTER 13

Initech

IN 2000, BRIDGE NINE TRIPLED ITS OUTPUT OVER PREVIOUS years, from releasing one record annually to three. I'd started the year with a split 7-inch EP that paired Jesse Standhard's new band, Right Brigade, with local punks A Poor Excuse, then spent most of my energy pushing the American Nightmare record. As the first anniversary of Ten Yard Fight's historic last show approached, I wrapped up the year with the label's first film release: a sixty-one-minute documentary about the band, culminating with scenes from their final performance the previous year. Hopes of releasing the VHS video at the second annual *Edge Day* show—which saw In My Eyes bow out in a similarly celebrated fashion as Ten Yard Fight had the previous October—were dashed due to manufacturing delays. Still, we were able to open up the evening with a full premiere of the film on the stage through a rented projector. I took preorder sales at the venue, and it came out six weeks later. At the time, it was one of the most professionally produced films documenting the live performance of a hardcore band, which helped attract a fair amount of attention to Bridge Nine. As In My Eyes closed out their contribution to Boston hardcore, the band passed the baton to American Nightmare.

Kurt Ballou had some studio time open for American Nightmare to record on short notice in November, so a month before they headed to LA, the band tracked three new original songs and covers of favorites from the Trouble and the Cro-Mags. The five-song release would come out the following March as *The Sun Isn't Getting Any Brighter* EP alongside two others, a Bridge Nine pressing of Shark Attack's originally self-released 7-inch and a proper LP vinyl pressing for Death Threat's *Peace & Security* album. In the meantime, I was heading to California to be the band's roadie; I wasn't going to miss their first shows on the West Coast. I'd heard great things about Carry On, a band from Los Angeles supporting the tour, and it would be my first chance to represent Bridge Nine on that side of the country.

My work with American Nightmare would eventually lead to the band signing with Equal Vision Records. Had that happened a year earlier when Tim had first sent in their demo, Bridge Nine would have missed the lighting-in-a-bottle moment of American Nightmare's first EP and all of the momentum that followed. The label likely would have grown to only a dozen or so releases, like the many labels that had started earnestly only to run out of steam within a few years. In those twelve months, I took a band with a lot of hype, added a distribution deal that put the release in stores across the country, and received personal guidance from the head of one of Boston's most popular indie labels—all the while funding it with a seemingly unlimited amount of cash diverted from sports fans. That was the recipe for my label's early success. Bands saw how I was investing in American Nightmare and hoped for similar treatment, as that kind of push was no longer available from most labels—the ones that had originally inspired mine because many of those labels had moved on to work with artists with more commercial appeal.

Carry On was one such band that could have fallen through the cracks. They performed just before American Nightmare, and I caught their set on the first night of American Nightmare's West Coast tour, held in the basement of a pizza restaurant in Bakersfield. Their performance blew me away. Their vocalist, Ryan George, had so much energy, bouncing around the stage and alternating between singing forcefully into the microphone, extending it into the audience, and then being overwhelmed by the crowd singing his lyrics back into his face as they crowded around him. And their guitar player, Todd Jones? He could write a serious guitar riff. I'd missed their earlier trip to the East Coast but had heard about how great they were from friends. After spending the next few days with the band and realizing we were all on the same page, I offered to release their first album. They agreed, and the following April, as I prepared to return to Fenway Park for my second season hawking "Yankees Suck" gear, I flew the band to Boston so that, like American Nightmare, they too could go into the studio with Kurt Ballou and work with Jacob Bannon on the design of their album.

If 2000 saw the launch of American Nightmare, 2001 was the year that kick-started the Bridge Nine label. I was fielding requests from dozens of bands and planned to work with many of them. Seemingly overnight, I had become a more significant player, and it went from me trying to meet new people to new people trying to meet me. A year earlier I was struggling to justify eating lunch out, and now I was flying bands all over the country. By the time Carry On entered the studio that spring, I'd committed to nine other bands as well, quadrupling the label's output from the previous year to twelve new releases. I had an LP in the works for the Berkley, California, band Breathe In, and new EPs for Boston's Cops and Robbers, the Hope Conspiracy, and Panic, a band that featured original ex–American Nightmare members Azy on guitar, Jesse on drums, and Gibby from the Trouble on vocals. I still didn't fully know what I was doing, but I worked my ass off and had some good luck go my way. In many regards, I was making it up as I went along—yet everything seemed to click.

Big Wheel was also growing quickly, and the responsibilities of my day job expanded with it. Rama's label gained momentum thanks to the commercial success of releases by indie-rock bands like Hot Rod Circuit and the (International) Noise Conspiracy. His most notable release at the time was a full-length album compilation of rare tracks by major-label emo influencers Jimmy Eat World.

Rama recruited Aaron Turner, who sang for the experimental-metal band Isis and was the founder of the Hydra Head Records label, to help him transition into his first commercial office space. Hydra Head had seen critical success over the previous year with the band Cave In's sophomore album, *Jupiter*, later ranked the second-best metal release of the decade by *Decibel* magazine, coming in behind *Jane Doe* by local favorites and Hydra Head alumni Converge. Hydra Head had help from co-owner Mark Thompson, who ran the day-to-day operation alongside Tortuga Recordings, his emerging label with a small roster of bands that complemented Hydra Head's. These labels were part of a growing collective of extreme-music record labels with roots in the Mission Hill neighborhood. Hydra Head and Tortuga operated out of the first floor of Aaron's three-bedroom Hillside Street apartment; shelves and stacks of CDs and vinyl releases filled what had been the living room and two of the bedrooms.

Rama, Aaron, and Mark all were tired of working from their respective apartments and needed a separation between their home and work lives. (Working at the Big Wheel loft office, I was almost always at my desk before Rama had even woken up; he'd come out of his room blinking, his eyes adjusting to the bright sunlight from the large factory-style windows, still half asleep as he entered the label side of the apartment in whatever he'd gone to bed in the night before.) They pooled their resources and started looking for a new location that fitted the businesses they were becoming. A shared, dedicated office space would provide that. Like the tech start-ups birthed from garages in the '90s and destined for shiny office buildings, it was time for them to leave their humblest abodes and step up the ladder. They eventually settled on an industrial office space on Boylston Street in the Fenway neighborhood, at the intersection of Yawkey Way (now Jersey Street), home to Fenway Park. Previously the longtime office of a building management and real-estate company for affordable housing to low-income families, the main lower level had no windows and was located below a Domino's Pizza restaurant and a sports-collectibles store run by the building's owner, with a smaller area upstairs next to the bathrooms. It wasn't particularly attractive, but it was an actual office, not someone's apartment, so it was a step up.

The space was in rough shape. In the basement, we removed the suspended ceiling to open things up and add a few inches, exposing a maze of plumbing pipes and electrical conduits. Rama rented a power sprayer to paint a bright shade of minty green over the dated, dark wood paneling. He and some friends put down a dark-green carpet; the results made it clear they had never installed one before. Big Wheel Recreation took over the larger office downstairs, while the second floor, which benefited from a giant wall of windows overlooking the parking spaces behind the building and enjoyed the only natural sunlight, became the new home of Hydra Head and Tortuga Recordings. There was only one doorway into the main office, with a stairwell connecting the underground world of Big Wheel's indie-pop to Hydra Head's realm of experimental heavy metal above. Thanks to a tip from a Big Wheel intern, we filled the office with used furniture rescued from a closing storage facility. Each person had their area cordoned off with orange-fabric cubicle partition walls, and a large oval conference table was in the center of the office. With everything in place, Rama christened the collaborative effort *Initech*, after the fictional (and dysfunctional) company featured in the movie *Office Space*.

Not only was Initech a step forward as a working environment, but it was also a chance to share everyday expenses, like roommates would to lower the cost of doing business for everyone involved. Now, there was only one fax machine phone line to pay for and just a single internet provider needed. We used our collective buying power to get better deals, stretching everyone's budgets further. We began reserving entire pages in magazines and splitting them with our ads. But when we figured out how to work together, we gained much more than savings. Initech took a bunch of really creative people used to working by themselves and put them together where they could interact with and learn from each other.

Suddenly, everyone had a larger sounding board and more people to brainstorm with. Even though we were different companies working with contrasting genres of music, our goals and pain points were the same: funding, record pressing and distribution, marketing, and promotion of our artists. Everyone was so excited about what they were working on that it was infectious and inspiring at the same time, with such a wealth of indie-music industry knowledge and contacts under one roof for all of us to tap into. I went in as an employee with only a dozen or so records, while Big Wheel and Hydra Head had collectively released more than one hundred. If I was tackling something new to me, odds were they had already dealt with it a half-dozen times. What started as a group of people who'd been working on their own began to coalesce into a team. I credit my time among that group of people as a big part of the education I needed.

Sales at Fenway Park had been profitable enough that first season to fund the American Nightmare release and cover my living expenses. But with multiple full-length albums planned for 2001, with all the bells and whistles that went along with a higher-profile production, I needed to ramp up things. The money was required up front to get these new bands into the studio, and it was upwards of six or more months before the money I was investing in them would return to me. The American Nightmare record sold well but was still just a low-priced EP. The 7-inch sold for five dollars in stores, and the CD was going for eight or nine bucks. I was getting less than half that from distributors and putting any of that money back into the band as quickly as it came in by taking out additional advertisements to keep getting the word out.

I knew I had captured only a fraction of the opportunity on the street in 2000. At least half of the people exiting the stadium appeared to walk past us and down into Kenmore Square, but there were also parking lots, the commuter rail station, and other exits all around the block. By putting additional vendors in those areas, I could increase my reach and earn more money than I had the previous season. I recruited more friends, and when the 2001 season home opener on April 6 kicked off, with Tim Wakefield on the mound for the Boston Red Sox against the Tampa Bay Devil Rays, we made sure we covered each corner of Fenway Park. Throughout that first home stand where Boston swept Tampa, I saw sales triple over my efforts a year earlier.

Expanding ground was only one part of the equation. I also needed to diversify my products. I quickly realized I could put "Yankees Suck" on anything and people would buy it. I was entertaining any ideas that could increase sales. Vinyl stickers and buttons were great impulse items with large profit margins, but so were embroidered patches, enamel pins, and even packages of temporary tattoos. I even made handheld flags, but had to preemptively remove their decorative yet sharply pointed tops before each game because security at the gates had begun confiscating them over concerns they'd be used as a weapon. If I'd been walking home with 700 or 800 bucks on an average night, I was now shoving more than $1,000 or more into my backpack after each game.

The work also came with some sacrifice. When the band Shark Attack announced that they were breaking up during a show stacked with the hardcore-punk genre-defining legends the Cro-Mags and Bad Brains, I had to leave the venue before they even got onstage. Their hometown team, the Philadelphia Phillies, was playing at Fenway that night. If I stayed at the show and skipped the postgame hustle, it would have been the same as me paying 1,000 bucks or more to see the band perform. With the label's expenses rapidly adding up, I was determined to do whatever necessary to ensure I could pay every bill that came in.

CHAPTER 14

Any Band

THE 2001 RED SOX TEAM WAS HELPED BY THE ARRIVAL OF designated hitter Manny Ramirez, who had just signed a $160 million deal with Boston for the next decade with one purpose: to beat the Yankees. This made him the highest-paid player on the team and rightfully so: he immediately delivered and had a .406 batting average during April, earning him the American League Player of the Month Award. Batting in the .400s was an almost unachievable goal: it meant he was getting on base more than four out of every ten times at bat. To anyone who needs some context, a batting average of .300 (getting on base three out of ten times) is considered excellent. That same month, Manny helped the Red Sox win a close Friday the thirteenth game against the Yankees by driving in two runs during the bottom of the tenth inning, firing the ball right between pitcher Mariano Rivera's legs. There wasn't a Sox fan still sitting in their seats, and chants of "Yankees suck!" barreled through the stadium as fans celebrated and the Yankees walked off the field with their heads down.

On-the-field heroics aside, when it came to the Red Sox and Yankees rivalry, it wasn't just the street vendors fanning the flames; players did as well. After shutting the Yankees out in a 3–0 win at Fenway and striking out thirteen batters over eight innings, Pedro Martínez responded to questions that had dogged him earlier in the season about his having come up short against the Yankees by responding, "I don't believe in curses. Wake up the damn Bambino and have me face him. Maybe I'll drill him in the ass." The *Boston Globe* printed the quote on the cover of the sports section, but the words proved hollow as Pedro's May 30 win would be the Red Sox's last against New York for the rest of the season. The Yankees once again had Boston's number.

By that summer, I wasn't able to handle the workload at both my day job and Bridge Nine, so I stepped down from my marketing position at Big Wheel. I kept my cluttered little cubicle and started paying rent for my corner in the Initech office. I had already moved most of Bridge Nine's inventory from my apartment and piled it to the ceiling around my desk, so thankfully, the days of my bedroom looking like a supply closet were behind me. The label had proved itself worthy with our new distributor, and we began paying for our share of the resources that all Initech-associated businesses depended on to operate.

I also brought the first person into the office to assist me with the ever-increasing list of responsibilities—Max Powers, a seventeen-year-old high school student. Yes, that's his real name, and he embodied it. I'd met Max two years earlier when he was doing a cut-and-paste, photocopied skateboard-centric fanzine called *Crete*. After seeing an ad promoting Bridge Nine's short-lived attempt at also making skate decks, he mailed me a copy. We corresponded a bit, and Bridge Nine became an advertiser in *Crete*, initially trading a skate deck for a half-page ad.

Max became a regular at hardcore shows and was friendly with Matt, the short-lived sticker hawker arrested outside Fenway earlier in the season. Matt introduced Max to Jesse Standhard, who recruited Max to work with him, first inside Fenway, giving free swag to people who signed up for credit cards, and later selling for the Suckers in May. By June, Max stopped by to pick up a Bridge Nine ad for the second issue of his new fanzine, *Not in Order*, and saw the Initech office for the first time.

Max was still a kid, but a go-getter. He had a hustle that I'd seen in only a few people. Upon arriving at the office, he asked if I needed help. I did. I struggled to keep up with fulfilling all the incoming mail orders, while lining up the new releases: from negotiating with bands to piecing the album designs together and making sure everything was put into production at the pressing plant on time. I agreed and immediately put him to work as the label's first intern, assembling records for Bridge Nine's latest signing, Breaker Breaker from San Francisco, a band with transplants from New England that included a guitarist who'd been in Proclamation. As the label's twelfth release, I pressed their five-song demo recording on 7-inch vinyl.

The timing of the move and recruiting of Max couldn't have been better. I'd spent the previous six years getting Bridge Nine's catalog up to eight releases, and I was about to add a dozen more over the next nine months. The label was no longer just me pressing records for my friends' bands; it had gained international attention and added artists from all over the country. I could have signed any band I wanted, and the roster continued growing.

Rama and Aaron were now available on a day-to-day basis and let me bounce questions off them, and I absorbed every tip and bit of info I could. They provided me with referrals for other places to press records, plants that did more exciting colors and patterns of vinyl than the limited palette of the first place I'd worked with. And best of all, I could piggyback on opportunities they'd earned and benefited from just by being there. For example, Lumberjack Distribution helped the Initech office collectively release a compilation CD titled *Make Like a Tree and Leave*, pairing Bridge Nine hardcore bands American Nightmare and Carry On with future emo-pop superstars Dashboard Confessional, the All-American Rejects, and Jimmy Eat World. They distributed the low-cost twenty-two-song disc through

Hot Topic stores nationwide, the same retail chain that had inadvertently funded some of the label's earliest singles by selling my novelty bumper stickers. That compilation became the first introduction to Bridge Nine, American Nightmare, and Carry On for way more people than I ever could have reached on my own.

Bridge Nine was no stranger to collaborating with friends, and I had become well versed in how helpful it can be to pool resources and work together toward a common goal. We built Initech on this principle, and those efforts continued outside our office. My favorite collaborators at the time were Tre McCarthy and Jacob Bannon via their newly christened Deathwish, Inc., label. Formed a year earlier by two veterans of the hardcore-punk scene, Tre was a career roadie for bands, and Jacob had been singing in the band Converge for a decade.

I met Tre shortly after moving to Boston in 1998. He was often on the road, so he rented the stairwell in the back of a house as a place to sleep and leave his stuff while he toured—the same apartment where I got my first tattoo. It had an upper landing that fitted a small mattress and had room for stacked milk crates to hold books, folded clothing, and a handful of possessions. Most people would think that renting a stairwell to sleep in was crazy, but that was the kind of sacrifice it took to let Tre tour and see the world with his friends' bands.

In 2001 shortly after forming their Deathwish label, Jacob and Tre approached me about releasing a promotional CD sampler with tracks from all the artists we were working with. Samplers were the go-to format for promoting new music, an annual staple for established labels to promote their rosters. The internet was too slow to conveniently download full albums, and everyone was still playing CDs. We had yet to release a free sampler, so the short-lived *Fighting Music* series was created. It pulled together tracks from Bridge Nine and Deathwish, as well as Toledo, Ohio–based Thorp Records, another hardcore-centric label run by an employee of our distrib-

ridge Nine's
edroom office
9 Sewall Street,
oston (1999)

Guerrilla marketing efforts around Boston . . .

Working in the Tower Records basement art department (1999)

. . . and across the Charles River (1999)

Waiting for the doors to open at TEN YARD FIGHT's "final" show (1999)

TEN YARD FIGHT covered in spray string at the end of their 10.17.99 performance (1999)

The Mission Hill crew's vendors fueling the rivalry (2000)

Chris Wrenn leaping off the speakers while CONVERGE performs at Hellfest (2000)

The Mission Hill "Yankees Suck" crew on the bridge to Fenway Park after a Red Sox game (2000)

Wes Eisold / AMERICAN NIGHTMARE (2000)

Chris Wrenn & Wes Eisold selling after a game (2000)

BOUT 00:59AM. OFFICERS COOPINGER AND MCCORMACK IN THE B101A UNIT RESPONDED TO A R/C
OR A MAN POSSIBLY SHOT AT 9 SEWALL ST.
VHILE ENROUTE OFFICERS WERE UPDATED THAT INDEED THERE WAS A VICTIM AND THAT [redacted] WAS AT
HE B&W HOSPITAL E.R. ROOM UPON ARRIVAL OFFICERS WERE MET BY THE B906 SGT. MERNER.
HE APARTMENT WERE EMPTY & SECURED AT 9 SEWALL ST.
GT MERNER DISCOVERED SMALL AMOUNTS OF BLOOD ON THE STREET AND SIDEWALK OPP. 9 SEWALL
SPOTS WERE MARKED AND A CRIME SCENE WAS ESTABLISHED. SGT MERNER THEN AMDE THE
OFICATIONS. A REPORT ON THE VICTIMS CONDITION WAS GIVEN TO THE OFFICERS BY DR. ZAWE AS
RITICAL. B-2 DETECTIVES INTERVIEWED WITNESSES AND OCCUPANTS OF 9 SEWALL ST. BOTH AT THE
OSPITAL AND AT THE CRIME SCENE. THE OCCUPANTS OF THE 1ST FLR. APARTMENT WHO WERE ALSO
ITNESSES ALLOWED OFFICERS TO ENTER THE BUILDING. EVIDENCE AND PHOTOS OF THE VICTIMS
PARTMENT WERE SEIZED AND SECURED. THE CRIME APPARENTLY TOOK PLACE IN THE VICTIMS [redacted]
[redacted] PERSONEL ON SCENE WERE AS FOLLOWS. B906 SGT. MERNER
101A OFFICER COPPINGER & MCCORMACK
K01A OFFICERS MISKELL & MCCARTHY
415A OFFICER FAYE, B425A OFFICER HARRIS
02 DETECTIVES B806 DET KENNEY, B801 DET BENTON, B823 DET WATERS.
OMICIDE DETECTIVES V902 SGT DET KEELER, V811 DET HARRIS PHTOGRAPHER VD 64 HARDY
ALLISTICS VD 25 CAMPER
ROM THE DA'S OFFICE MR. MAISAI MALIEK KING
S THE VICTIM APPERAS TO BE SUFFERING FROM A SINGLE GUN SHOT TO THE CHIN WHICH MAY HAVE
AMAGED [redacted] CARATOID ARTERY.
STED WITNESS DESCRIBED ALL 3 SUSPECTS AS BEING B/M'S ALL WEARING DK. CLOTHING WITH
OODIES MEDIUM TO HEAVY BUILDS RUNNING UP SEWALL ST TOWARDS DELLE AVE NOTHING
JRHTER.

IT ASSIGNED	SHIFT	REPORTING OFFICER'S NAME	REPORTING OFFICER'S ID	PARTNER'S ID
01A	1	RICHARD F. MCCORMACK	11050	11302

ECIAL UNITS NOTIFIED(REPORTING)
ea B-2

TE OF REPORT	TIME COMPLETED	APPROVING SUPERVISOR NAME	APPROVING SUPERVISOR ID
/04/2000	12:59 AM	GERARD W BAILEY	10502

MISSION HILL NEWS

ıme 8, Number 7 Circulation 4,000 November 22, 20

Students Assaulted

The shooting at 9 Sewall (2000), as covered in the local paper, *Mission Hill News*.

n Brookins

threatening attacks on Northeastern students in Mission Hi
gely missing from the Boston press. An upper division stude
as shot in the bedroom of his 9 Sewall Street apartment on
freshman student, whose name is being withheld was knife
October 22nd. We have been able to get eye witness accoun
October 22nd. We have been able to get eye witness accoun
at shooting or we would know very little about what happe

dditional coverage by locating the 56 officers we should be allocated to Missi
ill. A clash of cultures would seem to be occurring. The college residents and
e high school visitors to Mission Hill come from different worlds. We cove
e matter as a cautionary tale with for our new residents: Don't attempt to do
legal business with the locals

The INITECH crew (2002)

(L to R): Matt Galle, Aaron Power, Bryan Sheffield, Jen Malone, Mark Thompson, Chris Wrenn, Matt Pike

Selling anti-Yankees T-shirts on the bridge to Kenmore Square (2003)

Red Sox / Yankees coverage in the *New York Post* featured not just the teams, but the merch as well (2004)

On the field at Fenway, giving back for the first time (2004)

Bombers, Sox fans gear up for another showdown

Kevin P. Coughlin

N.Y. P

e Yankees begin a four-game stand against the Red S
ns of when they last won World Series (right) while So

y JENNIFER FERMINO *in Boston*
ınd BRIAN LEWIS *in New York*

Vith the New York Yankees' an-
al springtime trip to Fenway
k just days away, Bronx Bomber
s are predicting yet another
mmeling of their New England
h rivals.
The winners of 26 World Series
es will shuttle to Beantown Fri-
y to open a four-game set against
near-perennial runner-up Red
x.

Yankees consistently tr
Beantown brethren.
But Manhattanite An
didn't seem as confiden
Red Sox look strong.
"They've got a heck o
year," Cruz said of the
ways been a rivalry b
two of them."
Meanwhile, 250 miles
The Bronx, ever-frustra
fans were again hope
might be their year.
"When the Yankees

Ben Affleck showing off his Killin' With Schillin' T-shirt (2004)

PHOTO: MATT STONE

Old habits die hard, guerrilla marketing effort (2003)

ERTY OF YANKEE - HATER DOT COM GoSOX

HAVE HEART's "final" show on 10.17.09 (2009)

Friends wore "HAVE HEART SUCKS" T-shirts after the band performed a sold-out show to over 2,000 people (2009)

PHOTOS: TODD POLLOCK

utor, Lumberjack. We didn't have enough new music by ourselves to justify our own samplers, so compiling the tracks allowed us to split the cost three ways, ultimately ensuring that we'd distribute three times more copies than we could afford to make on our own and leveraging each other's audiences. Jacob asked tattoo artist Mike Lussier to illustrate the cover, and we had them ready to start handing out at the Boston-area stop of the 2001 Vans Warped Tour.

Eight of the twelve new records released on Bridge Nine in 2001 were slated to come out between October and November alone. I spent the spring and summer getting bands into studios and working with them on the artwork. I published my own Bridge Nine fanzine and interviewed all of our bands, distributing ten thousand copies for free. They were included in every mail order, and I gave boxes of them to bands to take on tour and shipped others to record stores around the country to leave out for their customers. I designed and submitted the ads, while Max worked to put together a street team of fans in other cities that could help us spread the word. It was a significant increase in every aspect of what I'd been doing at the label until that point. I spent most of my days at the Initech office working and my nights down the street selling swag to Red Sox fans after every game. The move to the new space helped facilitate hawking at Fenway Park because I was now only two blocks away instead of a mile. Instead of lugging everything down to the park each game in Elisabeth's red Ford Mustang and driving in circles to find parking, I could keep working at the label while I waited for my crew of friends to meet up at the office before walking over.

I'd pass out their bags, signs, and a few envelopes of stickers, fifty in each, and then we'd walk across the street to Fenway Park when the sixth inning came around. Every home stand was a marathon, and you couldn't judge how things were going based on a single game. Many variables could affect sales on any given day: rain delays, getting chased by Codees, and the game getting blown out in the early innings. I preferred close games where

Boston lost at the last moment over games where they dominated the other team because close games meant more butts in seats until the ninth inning, and we always did better when most people stayed until the end.

We knew people didn't typically feel comfortable walking up to a lone street vendor at night; we had better odds of attracting and keeping a crowd when everyone was leaving at once. Often when people seemed hesitant to stop, I'd pretend to be a customer for my vendors, standing in front of them, rubbing my chin while appearing to be deciding what to buy, and the ruse usually attracted a few legitimate buyers behind me.

On August 31, 2001, the Red Sox were eight games behind the Yankees after falling to them in the first three-game series at Fenway, of which they lost all three. The Sox headed to Cleveland, where they took only one of three games, and then went to the Bronx for another round, where they were swept once again. By September 10, Boston was an embarrassing fourteen games behind the Yankees, and Red Sox fans were jumping like rats from a sinking ship. During that first home stand of September with New York, the abuse hurled at us was off the charts. Die-hard Sox fans had admitted defeat, and we found them trying to argue with us over whether the Yankees actually sucked as they walked by. Sales plummeted, and it became clear that despite having enjoyed almost two full seasons of exponential growth, our singularly focused collection wasn't exempt from a market correction.

As it turns out, *a market correction* was the understatement of the century.

CHAPTER 15

Nine-Eleven

TUESDAY, SEPTEMBER 11, 2001. THE FREE-SPIRITED DAYS OF crapping on New York over a sports rivalry were over, at least for the rest of the 2001 baseball season. Terrorists flew two planes out of Boston's Logan Airport into one of the most iconic locations in New York City, the Twin Towers of the World Trade Center. The attack was an unprecedented tragedy, the worst seen on US soil since Pearl Harbor, and it united everyone against a common enemy during a time that saw petty sports rivalries go by the wayside. In the wake of 9/11, no one had a bad thing to say about New York—which had been the foundation of my business model. Almost everything I offered took shots at the Yankees, and I was on the verge of being out of business overnight. Like the rest of the country, I was outraged and saddened by this tragedy; from a purely practical business perspective, I was also kind of fucked.

When the Yankees finally returned to the field on September 18 at Comiskey Park in Chicago for a game against the White Sox, local fans held up a twelve-foot-wide hand-painted sign that read "Chicago Loves NY, God Bless America." The entire nation shared that sentiment, and Boston was no exception. On September 24, in the middle of the fourth inning when Detroit was in town, a near-capacity crowd inside Fenway Park stood on their feet and sang along to a recording of Frank Sinatra's "New York, New York." Such a song would have been greeted with a boisterous "Yankees suck" chant just two weeks earlier, but fans sang along with the same enthusiasm usually reserved for Neil Diamond's "Sweet Caroline," an eighth-inning tradition.

The effect on our inventory was immense; we couldn't give it away. Before the terrorist attack, we already had trouble moving product during games when the Red Sox were behind the Yankees by double digits. If I was going to salvage what was left of the 2001 season, I needed to pivot.

Bumper stickers, my bread-and-butter at the park, took a few weeks to come in from my West Coast printer, but I could have T-shirts made down the street on a day's notice. With fans becoming hyperpatriotic—and my need to diversify with something that didn't target New York—I opted to run with something that pandered to the crowd: I took a photo of Osama bin Laden, the prime suspect behind the attacks, and designed an Old West–style poster with "Wanted: Dead or Alive," crossing out "Alive" and adding "Dead" handwritten next to it. This tapped into the fervent pro-America sentiment that gripped the nation after weeks of twenty-four-hour news cycles naming bin Laden as the culprit and kept me afloat. With the imminent release of eight Bridge Nine albums, the bills were stacking up. My manufacturing expenses alone added up to more than $50,000 for October. This pressure was exacerbated by the fact that the Red Sox would ultimately be eliminated from postseason contention; Sox fans (and the rest of the world) would go on to watch the Yankees head to their thirty-eighth appearance in the World Series.

The 2001 World Series was the first to end in November due to the season postponement after the 9/11 attacks. Despite most people outside of Massachusetts hoping New York would win, they were ultimately beaten in a dramatic seven-game series by the Arizona Diamondbacks. Before they even threw the first pitch, I was on a plane with American Nightmare to Amsterdam to start their first European tour.

Wes was the son of a career naval officer and had lived in Germany when he was younger, but traveling to Europe was a first for the rest of us. It still fascinated me that the opportunity to explore the world was made possible because he and Tim had written ten songs over the previous year in our Mission Hill apartment. Tim's guitar riffs were good, and Wes had an incredible way with words, but together they made a band that was greater than the sum of its parts. Their efforts allowed us to bounce all over Europe and the United Kingdom for the next three weeks. Few hardcore bands were as highly anticipated as American Nightmare was on their inaugural trip, and only a handful have matched the excitement in the decades since.

We were met at the airport by Johan and Suzanne, who owned Reflections Records. Their Dutch hardcore label was comparable in size to Bridge Nine and had licensed both EPs as a compilation titled *Year One*. It was Bridge Nine's first licensing deal. Having someone in Europe promoting and making the recordings more widely available was a massive boost for the band and helped bring them to tour. Reflections artists Reaching Forward supported the tour on the mainland Europe dates, and the brand-new English band Sworn In was on the three UK dates. It was Sworn In's first show ever, and I was there to see it happen.

We stared in awe from the windows of the tour van as we made our way from city to city. Winding across the countryside of Belgium, up through the mountains of the Italian Alps, on the cold and windy ferry across the North Sea to Sweden. Before their show in Zurich, Switzerland, the band and I entered a Swiss bank, where I tried to open an account. That's what international businesspeople did, right? And I had a business that had gone international. But I was informed that I needed to deposit $10,000 to open the account, and most of my money was sitting in a safe at the bottom of my closet—I didn't even have a business bank account on American soil yet—so there went that idea.

As American Nightmare's merch seller in a pre-Euro currency market, I was tasked with learning the exchange rate of each new country we visited, with assistance from a member of the opening band as we stocked our tables each night. I had pressed a special edition of American Nightmare's *The Sun Isn't Getting Any Brighter* 7-inch on purple vinyl for the tour, which ended up selling out. European punks paid a king's ransom for special editions of records released in the United States, and this was their chance to gain leverage in trades with American fans. Between that vinyl and the band's four T-shirt designs, running the merch table was a whirlwind almost every night. I brought a suitcase full of Bridge Nine releases and sold them across Europe, meeting people and spreading awareness for the label in a way I couldn't have done back home in the States, which was a great time.

Traveling in the months after 9/11 was, of course, also stressful. Just two weeks before we headed to Europe—touring under the name *American Nightmare*, mind you—the war in Afghanistan had begun. Air strikes were launched by US and British forces against Taliban and al-Qaeda training camps, and the ground war started the week before the tour. Americans abroad were seen as targets.

While the tour stopped in England, an additional stress was added by the news of American Airlines Flight 587, which crashed on November 12 in a Queens, New York, neighborhood. It killed all 260 people on the plane and 5 on the ground, making it the second deadliest aviation incident in US history. Though we would later learn that the crash resulted from a crew member's error, terrorism was immediately suspected (and not ruled out until months later), and we were flying back to the United States the following week. On top of that, Bridge Nine and its eight new releases were left in the hands of a teenage Max Powers, who'd only started working in the office months earlier. Anxiety was high and I was feeling it acutely, but I was doing my best to hold it together. With help from Elisabeth, Max kept things running in my absence, and the lights were still on when I returned.

CHAPTER 16

Hustle

RUMORS OF THE RED SOX GOING ON THE AUCTION BLOCK TO the highest bidder had circulated for years, and by late 2001, the opportunity to buy the team and their Fenway Park home formally opened. The highest amount paid for a baseball team had been set two years earlier when the Cleveland Indians (now Guardians) sold for $323 million, and the Red Sox were expected to blow that figure out of the water, a significant increase from the $20 million that the current owner had paid just twenty-three years earlier. That wouldn't be good news for the street hustle, because just like in the late 1970s when the Red Sox sold for a record amount, the new owners would no doubt clamp down on anyone else trying to make a buck around the stadium on their watch.

The winning bid more than doubled the highest amount paid for a team at $660 million, bought by a team of investors that included John Henry, a quiet yet extraordinarily successful businessman and baseball-club owner who briefly controlled the Florida Marlins—a team he would need to sell to help make the Sox deal happen. With an estimated net worth of almost $1 billion, John Henry wasn't just a member of the 1 percent; he also owned

1 percent of the New York Yankees. Purchased in 1991 for $1 million, it was his first stake in a Major League Baseball team. With his clear conflict of interest as an owner of the Red Sox, John Henry sold his interest and earned a $6.3 million profit while having enjoyed all of the perks of being a "minority shareholder" for a decade.

Part of what made John Henry's bid so attractive was that his group of investors planned to renovate Fenway Park, modernizing the facility and increasing seating capacity. This plan was opposed to building a new stadium elsewhere in the city—a heavily debated topic and something for which the previous ownership group had been pushing. By the 2002 season, Fenway Park was the oldest venue in baseball at ninety years of age and didn't offer many of the conveniences and comforts that came with modern ballparks. The seats were too small, and some areas had obstructed views. But legends had played on that field—Babe Ruth, Jimmie Foxx, Ted Williams—and the stadium's history was priceless. Walking the same concourses as the greats was part of the Fenway Park experience—a connection to the past that was getting rarer in baseball. Chicago's Wrigley Field, built in 1914, is the only other ballpark from that era still in use. The next oldest was Dodger Stadium, constructed fifty years after Fenway Park. There was no comparison. Many were thankful that John Henry's group of investors had won the bid, but I remained concerned about how it would affect my business.

Meanwhile, Initech mastermind Rama Mayo left Boston to bring Big Wheel Recreation to the West Coast, opening an office in Los Angeles. His label maintained a presence in Boston with Aaron Power, a music-loving Northeastern University student, at the helm. Friends Matt Pike and Matt Galle, who until this point had been booking tours for bands out of their apartments, brought their newly formed Kenmore Booking Agency into the fold. They named their company after the square a few blocks away and took over Rama's vacant office space. Jen Malone's public relations company, Black & White, moved in down the hall from Hydra Head, and Ohio-based Doghouse Records hired photographer Bryan Sheffield to run their East Coast satellite operation from our office. At its peak, Initech housed seven music businesses with five record labels spanning a diverse spectrum of independent music and representing artists worldwide. It was a unique coalition later chronicled in *Alternative Press* and *Revolver* magazines, and it earned several appearances in the *Boston Globe* newspaper, including a "Living Arts" section cover story about our collaborative work environment.

The post–9/11 moratorium on Yankee hating was brief, and Boston fans resumed another season of rooting against New York louder than they did for the home team. In case there were still hard feelings, I brought out an "I Love New York, but I Hate the Yankees" bumper sticker to add to the spread and appeal to both sentiments. I sent six or more vendors out each game night with courier bags full of stickers, patches, and pins, and people from all over the country who had traveled to Boston to see their team play the Red Sox were buying up the swag. Back then there was no "I'll order that online later." You bought it when you saw it or regretted it on your way home.

Going into the spring of 2002, Bridge Nine's sound diversified with its first decidedly more traditional "rock" release by Sinners & Saints, the alter ego of Blood for Blood's primary songwriter Rob Lind. The roster grew to include releases from bands that had played with American Nightmare on their first overseas tour, Britain's Sworn In and Holland's straight-edge export Reaching Forward. Stateside, we collaborated with Washington, DC's Striking Distance; paired Death Threat with our friends from San Diego, Over My Dead Body, on a split single; and licensed another split from the respected Jade Tree label with our friends in Kill Your Idols and Good Riddance. I then signed Seattle's Champion, which Tim had brought to my attention, saying they got the best crowd reaction from any band American Nightmare had played with on their latest tour.

The workload got heavier. Gone were the free-spirited days of chilling with my friends on Newbury Street. Now I was traveling with them and their bands all over the country and Europe, so I couldn't exactly complain. But I no longer had time to myself where I didn't *need* to be anywhere or *doing* anything anymore. It was getting to the point that there was always something I could be doing to push the label forward, and if I was doing anything else, it was taking away from that. I needed to find balance.

Max was a great help, working part-time on the books, but his availability was limited to afternoons when he got out of high school. So I offered Desmond Connolly, Bridge Nine's part-time remote webmaster, a full-time gig in the office to pick up the slack. The Bridge Nine staff was up to three. The release schedule that year was pretty consistent, but the fall had the heavy hitters and an equally substantial number of responsibilities.

American Nightmare was fast becoming one of the biggest hardcore-punk bands in the world. Their full-length album *Background Music* had been out for a year on Equal Vision, and they were selling out shows everywhere. In September 2002 they performed at the Worcester Palladium as part of the venue's annual Skatefest music festival. Toward the end of the song "Hearts," as Wes began to sing the lyrics "All I wanted was a shot in the dark . . . ," came a loud snapping sound, and the power to the venue went out, cloaking the entire stage and audience in complete darkness. The music stopped, but the crowd sang louder and finished the song in unison. Hundreds of voices joined in. I *still* get chills thinking about it.

November 26 had four big releases lined up for the same day, including a new album from Minneapolis's Holding On and a debut EP from Ramallah, another of Rob Lind's musical projects (for which I offered a record deal based solely on Rob's description that it was heavier than Blood for Blood). No Warning returned with their juggernaut *Ill Blood* LP, and Boston hardcore legends Slapshot got a stateside release for their *Greatest Hits, Slashes and*

Crosschecks album on CD. Now a rising player in the hardcore-punk scene, Bridge Nine's catalog was more than thirty releases deep.

Terror, hailing from Los Angeles, was the most talked about hardcore band in the country, and after going back and forth between Bridge Nine and another label on the West Coast, they'd finally agreed to work with me. The band featured two members of Carry On: guitar player Todd Jones and drummer Nick Jett, with Buffalo native Scott Vogel of Despair and Buried Alive on vocals. Oddly, the band had been set in motion by John Lacroix as his new post–Ten Yard Fight project, but he had backed out before the first practice. I later learned Scott was inspired to join the band after being given a cassette tape with the Carry On album I'd released on side A and the first No Warning EP on side B. Terror recorded their debut nine-song *Lowest of the Low* EP in a Cleveland studio in September with a January release date planned.

When that record came out, it became evident to me that I needed even more support. Signing Terror immediately put the attention of people from all over the world on us, and I was struggling to keep everything moving with our small crew. Desmond had recently met a guy named Darren and thought he could help. Darren was interested in what we were doing and initially just started coming to the office, hanging out, offering advice, and helping here and there. He was a fan of the music, was from New York City, and seemed sharp, so after he'd been chipping in for a few weeks, I added him to the payroll.

Darren's earliest contribution was in negotiating better terms from our manufacturers. The label had a lot of new releases in the works, but I had been using the same CD broker and hadn't asked enough questions to get the best pricing. Darren took over and started shopping our projects around. He was a fast talker who could make anything sound bigger and more impressive than it was, and it worked; we got better pricing and rushed service. He had one company doing the packaging and another duplicating and assembling the CDs, and they tripped over themselves to get our jobs turned around quickly.

This was all great, but at times felt too good to be true. Darren was promising future work that I knew we couldn't deliver. He was a great salesman, but how he went about it didn't feel honest. But too many new artists and releases were in the works that needed my attention, and as I endeavored to keep up, I decided to trust him rather than ask too many questions.

Bridge Nine continued to gain ground in Europe as I returned that November, a year after my first visit, this time with Slapshot. Working and touring with Slapshot was a big deal—it was the first time I'd collaborated with a band I had been a fan of before starting the label. Vocalist Jack "Choke" Kelly was a part of the original "Boston Crew," the group of friends that kick-started the hardcore-punk scene in Boston in the early 1980s. If not for their efforts twenty years earlier, my label and its bands wouldn't have looked or sounded the same. Having the opportunity to bring Jack into the fold was meaningful and symbolic. Slapshot was also a significantly bigger band in Europe than back home, so it helped solidify Bridge Nine's overseas standing and brought attention to the label from new international fans.

Meanwhile, the 2002 Red Sox season had ended with Boston ten and a half games behind the American League East–winning Yankees, who'd had 103 wins and only 58 losses that year. New York won their first postseason game but lost the next three and was eliminated in the American League Divisional Series by the wild card–winning Anaheim Angels. The Angels beat the Minnesota Twins in the Championship Series and ultimately bested the San Francisco Giants to win the World Series, their first in franchise history. It was the first time the Yankees did not make it to the World Series since 1997.

Boston had held their own for most of the season, ending with a record of 93 wins and 69 losses, but it was still a grind for the vendors toward the end, with the Yankees so far ahead in the standings. The Yankees took ten of their nineteen matchups with the Red Sox throughout the season. As the dust settled after getting spanked by Anaheim, they started making postseason moves to beef up their pitching, as they'd been leading every game in the American League Division Series (ALDS) until the later innings, when they proceeded to get blown out.

In December 2002, the Yankees edged the Red Sox out and signed rising star (and Cuban defector) José Contreras. Red Sox president Larry Lucchino was pressed for comment on Christmas Eve by the *New York Times* and responded, "The Evil Empire extends its tentacles even into Latin America," comparing the Yankees to the fictional antagonists of the *Star Wars* universe and branding them with a new nickname. Losing out on a chance to sign José gave Boston fans another reason to hate the Yankees as they awaited the start of the new season.

On Opening Day of the 2003 season, I walked up the stairs and out the back door of the Boylston Street office, the strap of my black courier bag resting on my shoulder. It was packed with stickers, the handle of my sign sticking out the side of the bag. It still felt like winter; the cold air stung my face as I pulled my sweatshirt hood over my head. My breath was visible each time I exhaled, the temperature was barely supposed to make it out of the thirties, and rain was forecast. All signs pointed to it being a bust at Fenway Park that day. I'd been preparing my return for months, plans for well over a dozen releases on Bridge Nine were in motion, and that annual infusion of baseball-fan cash was sorely needed, so I trekked to Fenway anyway to earn whatever money I could.

Suddenly, I heard a muffled Boston accent exclaim: "Ah-ha! So this is the hideout!" The captain of the Codees, Tiger's older brother, stood on the sidewalk, figuring he'd caught me in the act.

"You just realized this now?" I laughed. "We've been here for almost two years!"

I didn't know if he randomly stumbled upon me or if he was acting on intel. The game started at 2:05 p.m., which was still a few hours away, and he was on the wrong side of Fenway Park. It was well before the 8:00 p.m. time when vendors were allowed to be out, but I hadn't yet done anything that warranted being stopped. I continued on my way, wanting to get there early to see who else would be out and to watch the streets around the park come alive for the first time in months.

Large beer trucks were double-parked, and kegs were unloaded down aluminum ramps and lined up on the sidewalk. Fans were already making their way to the stadium. Sausage carts were rolled from the backs of trailers. They pushed into position along Lansdowne Street, and the Sausage King vendors handed their trademark nine-inch sausages over the cart counter outside of Gate E on Lansdowne Street to a pair of fans.

The lucky few, with their grandfathered-in stationary-vendor licenses, carefully placed Red Sox souvenirs on card tables as they curated their pennants, sweatshirts, and packages of baseball cards. Program hawkers in red shirts held magazines over their heads, standing with big round buttons that read "$2" fastened to their shirts, selling the programs one at a time while perched on a milk crate as fans walked by. Despite the cold, the crowds started to form, and I looked around to see if any of the usual suspects were out. It was a Friday morning, so my regular crew of hawkers was unavailable, either in class or at work. I wanted to grab some sales to make it worth my time. Code-enforcement details had become more common during the prior season, so I had to steer clear of the Captain, Tiger, and their crew of Codees before setting up shop.

I stopped in front of the bank at the edge of Kenmore Square, next to a little parking lot where an enterprising attendant managed to stuff twenty cars into about eight spaces each game. A steady flow of people walking by guaranteed plenty of interest while keeping me shielded from the street where a Codee's car would no doubt pass by at some point. In that event, I would stuff the sign back into my bag, a bright-red Sox hat would go on my head, and I would blend in with the rest of the fans walking over the bridge to Fenway Park.

Thankfully, there was no need for a disguise. I noted anyone else who was—and wasn't—out making money. The dark overcast sky, cold weather, and midday start time were likely a deterrent to some, but my office was just two blocks from the park. A cold drizzle eventually began to fall, so I started to pack up; bumper stickers didn't fare well in the rain. The vendors selling ponchos stood to be the clear winners that day, and I walked past the stadium back to the office with the hood of my sweatshirt pulled tight, the faint sound of the legendary Ray Charles singing "America the Beautiful" emanating from the park as part of the Opening Day ceremony. The game was ultimately postponed because of the rain, so a doubleheader was scheduled for the following day—a best-case scenario for me, as it added an extra game during which to sell.

Being out on Opening Day was more about sizing up the competition and seeing if anyone else had spent the offseason preparing to hit the streets as I had just a few years earlier. The threat of rain and the early game start time had kept Fenway relatively quiet, and only the regulars were out. The next day would be the test: the first game was at 1:05 p.m., and the temperature would be in the high fifties. A Saturday game and perfect weather for a springtime doubleheader meant anyone hoping to cash in would be there. Many of those people didn't know that the city restricted hawking during day games, and even if they had done their homework to obtain a peddler license, it wasn't valid during an afternoon game. Over the years I had watched plenty of people on Opening Day have everything they brought confiscated by Codees. The latter were happy to throw some poor sap's entrepreneurial dream into the trunk of their code car as evidence. That, coupled with a $200 fine, made most people realize that whatever they thought would happen selling at Fenway wouldn't be worth the effort.

Over time, I had unexpectedly started to build a bit of a rapport with Tiger. While the rest of the Codees seemed to relish catching us in the act and looked down on us with disdain, Tiger thought what we were doing was cool.

We were running around trying to make money whenever we could, and the rest of the Codees went out of their way, sometimes to a surprising degree, to try to stop us. Ultimately, we had nothing against them; they were doing their job, and we were doing ours. We kept the same schedules, and neither of us was in the streets because we wanted to be; it was just how we both paid the bills. They got their lucrative detail check, and we cashed in with baseball fans.

One afternoon as I was cutting through the Kenmore subway station, I unexpectedly made eye contact with Tiger as I walked up the stairs onto the street. He looked at me and slowly shook his head to say no. I took the hint, turned right around, and walked back down the stairs, ready to run over to the other side of the park as far away as possible from the Codee activity. I later learned he'd been on patrol with reinforcements, and his tipping me off had saved me a significant hassle.

Maybe he didn't want to deal with the paperwork involved. Or there were other people he could bust, giving a pass to the usual suspects he'd watched grind it out for a couple of years. But my gut said he knew we weren't going anywhere, and we might as well get along while we were all on the same few blocks game after game. Regardless, he treated me differently than others (as well as how he'd treated me before), with less resentment. After all this time coexisting at games, we began to get to know and see each other as people and not just cat versus mouse or, in this case, Tiger versus vendor. We'd stand in Kenmore Square several nights a week, shooting the shit after the crowds petered out. I learned that he had kids and this job was what he had to do to make ends meet. He was working the Codee details on top of his day job and stayed late at Fenway Park several times a week to work an overnight security shift inside. He was even delivering pies for a local pizza shop. I respected this man's hustle.

I told him about how the money I was earning funded my record label. He didn't seem interested in the music, but the surrounding scene and culture intrigued him.

"What about the Suckers?" Tiger inquired, referring to Rod and Worm's outfit. "Those dudes are just high-rolling until the ride ends," I replied.

Hearing that, Tiger chuckled. "The word coming down from the top is that street vending is funding organized crime and terror groups."

It was my turn to laugh. "Well, they've got it backward," I said. "I recently signed a group from LA named Terror, and Red Sox fans just helped me buy them a tour van."

I learned to appreciate Tiger's no-fucks-given attitude. He was prone to saying whatever was on his mind, not holding anything back. Truthfully, while he was a 100 percent proud Dorchester townie, he was more punk in spirit than many of the punks I knew.

As things became less combative, our collective was more willing to work with the Codees. First, we agreed to move back a little farther outside the scope of Fenway Park's surveillance cameras so security couldn't see us; therefore, they called code enforcement a lot less. Tiger and I also traded phone numbers to reach each other directly when necessary. I'd become the go-to guy for both crews, so he'd give me a call when they caught heat for us being too close to the park. I'd give him a heads-up when someone new we'd never seen before showed up to sell. It was mutually beneficial: the Codees got an easy bust, and we eliminated some competition before they could dig in.

I rolled down with six people, looking for places to post up and start fueling another season of Yankee hating. Unfortunately, rain was in the forecast until early afternoon, so the second attempt at an opening game was still up in the air. Fans were low-energy, but we still hustled to make whatever sales we could. We worked in groups of two: one person held a limited amount of product and sold it to fans, while the other kept an eye out for Codees and potential trouble while carrying the overstock. That allowed one person to engage with the crowd and not stress about Codees sneaking up on them, and on the off-chance they did, the inventory confiscated would be minimal. This practice also gave us a leg up on the guys selling shirts; they were sitting ducks when Codees rolled up on them, whereas we could disappear into the crowd.

Saturday's early attempt at a game was postponed because of the rain, but the second game of the doubleheader was still on. The temperature rose back into the sixties—that crazy up-and-down weather is typical in Boston during spring. The Suckers marched up with their boxes of shirts.

The season's first night game was a significant stake-your-territory moment, holding on to any ground we had gained in the previous year. Eight p.m. was the first moment that we could legally sell, assuming Codees were around to enforce it, but we ensured we were there early to stand in position. Shirt guys would have a garbage bag covering their boxes, ready to pull it off as soon as it was 8:00 p.m. If new vendors rolled up, this was a clear message that the spaces were spoken for and to keep moving deeper into Kenmore Square, farther from Fenway Park. As the clock ticked closer to 8:00, one thing stood out: no sign of the 21-ers.

The Sox started the game by giving up three earned runs to the Orioles. Sox pitching ace Pedro Martínez was on the mound and was getting uncharacteristically knocked around by a team that had come in fourth place in the American League East the previous season, with a crappy sub-.500 record of only sixty-nine wins and ninety-five losses. By the top of the fifth inning, Baltimore's bats showed no mercy, earning an additional seven runs before Pedro was pulled from the game to the uncharacteristic sound of boos as he walked off the field. It may have been the season opener with all of the pageantries that come with it, but that alone wasn't enough to keep people in their seats. A steady stream of disappointed fans headed for the exits early in the game, pausing on their way to the subway to tell us that despite our "Yankees Suck" signs saying otherwise, it was the Red Sox that sucked.

That first home stand saw the Red Sox go on to win seven of the remaining eight games, and at no point did the 21-ers return. It was a welcome change: having one less adversary to deal with was a relief. They probably realized there were easier ways to make money that didn't involve fighting with us over every square inch of sidewalk around Fenway Park.

With the 21-ers seemingly out of the picture, there was an opening in the market, and I felt after three years of street vending I'd earned the opportunity to fill it. I had collectively sold more than one hundred thousand bumper stickers, embroidered patches, enamel pins, and buttons to fans as they left Fenway Park. I'd kept away from T-shirts out of respect for Worm, as he had been the first of us to do it, making exceptions only here and there when a time-sensitive opportunity presented itself or if I couldn't get stickers from my West Coast printer quickly enough. I'd carved out my niche with the small products and had done well with them and was more or less content with what I was earning. That is—until the 21-ers threw in the towel.

By not offering shirts, I lost some of my better vendors to the Suckers' crew, as they had been making less money than the least competent T-shirt hawkers. T-shirts had more significant commission potential, and I needed to adapt or continue to lose talent. I was also facing sticker competition that I hadn't anticipated. Rock radio station WBCN 104.1, headquartered a block from Fenway Park, noticed the popularity of my bumper stickers. They regularly made concert-themed swag with their call letters to give away to listeners, and for about a week, I had to deal with them flooding the streets with free "Yankees Suck" stickers. It was like trying to sell cups of water next to a drinking fountain. Harassing some nineteen-year-old street teamer over it was the last thing I wanted to deal with, so I decided to diversify to protect myself.

Bridge Nine was supporting heavy-hitting albums by No Warning, Ramallah, and Slapshot and had recently unleashed the debut EP by Terror. I was about to spend $3,000 on Terror's first music video, directed by my friend Ian McFarland of the band Blood for Blood. The expenses continued to add up. If selling shirts brought in more money, I could invest it in putting out more records.

I watched Worm's crew happily and proudly piss away their money on drugs, gambling, designer clothes, and jewelry. The Suckers pretending to live large while they had the cash was an act of high-roller cosplay. I could have spent the money I earned on myself, but I was trying to build something. Maybe I should have bought a car or put a down payment on a condo, something to improve my means. But I didn't. I wanted to release more punk-rock records. I didn't see it as additional competition; I would maintain the status quo by replacing something that existed before Worm was on the scene. After the Red Sox headed southwest to take on the Texas Rangers at their Globe Life Park, I acted.

When I told Worm I planned to fill the void left by the 21-ers by adding shirts, he didn't take it well and definitely didn't see it as I did. He accused me of coming after his stake and wouldn't listen as I explained that I didn't want what *he* had; I wanted what the 21-ers were leaving behind. I didn't see the problem, as Worm was spending less time at the park, and Jesse Standhard was handling most of the day-to-day operation for the Suckers. People who had joined later were getting better opportunities. Several members of his current crew had initially come into the Fenway hustle through me; a few were in Bridge Nine bands. I had fought as hard as anyone to establish and protect what we were doing, and despite Worm not liking what he saw as new competition, I wouldn't budge.

Overnight, an additional rivalry at Fenway Park was born, now between two Mission Hill T-shirt hawkers vying for every dollar from baseball fans. This caused Worm to hate me, which was unfamiliar territory because I wasn't known to make enemies. I was, however, someone who jumped on opportunities, and if the 21-ers were leaving their piece of the pie on the table, I would take it for myself. Worm made it clear that he and I weren't cool anymore, but if keeping things cool with him meant forfeiting thousands of dollars every month, then I couldn't afford his friendship. I could sense Worm wanted to fight me over it one night as we walked past each other on the bridge after a game, but he didn't have the social capital to do anything. He knew I was tight with everyone else in the crew, and raising his fist was just an empty, frustrated threat. It bummed me out that he responded the way he did, but over the years, it became clear that Worm only ever looked out for himself, so it shouldn't have been a surprise.

My first T-shirts for Fenway were printed by the end of April and catered directly to Red Sox fans, with "F the Yanks" continuing the shot taking at Boston's New York rivals and "Boston Pride" over a pair of crossed baseball bats for those who were over the Yankee bashing. Bridge Nine was already ordering a lot of shirts from a local screen-printing shop for our bands, so I had good leverage and pricing.

Though I had thought sales were good with stickers, the money was immediately better selling shirts. In April, I had pulled in just shy of 8,000 bucks selling stickers, but I managed to nearly double that in May once I started hawking shirts, grossing more than $15,000. The expenses the label incurred to promote the bands were stacking up: $1,000 for a half-page ad promoting Terror in a mainstream heavy-metal magazine, six weeks of radio promotion at 300 bucks a pop, cash advances to bands for new equipment and tour support. As fast as the money was coming in, I was finding new ways to spend it, but I didn't consider any of it wasted. High-profile ads were putting these bands' names in front of new fans. A radio push meant a larger audience was hearing their songs. Good equipment and the ability to tour ensured they were on the road playing shows and building awareness for their bands, which translated to higher album sales.

The move into T-shirts came with additional headaches. They were easily stained and stolen, took up more space, and were more cumbersome to move and display. I was also ordering a thousand of each design at a time, and those costs needed to be covered up front. The investment was higher, but the margins were great. I was paying $3 each for a shirt and selling them for 10 bucks. I pulled in upwards of $2,000 a night and stashed away more money after a ten-game home stand than I'd had in my life. I was counting the cash after every game, and it was taking up more and more of my time—not that I minded. Laying $20 bills on each other repeatedly and counting to $1,000 before starting the next pile, and then the next, had a euphoric feel. I still didn't have a bank account for the label and keeping the money in a safe in my apartment became a liability, so I rented a safety deposit box at a bank close to Fenway Park, notably the only one I hadn't been laughed out of three years earlier, and kept my earnings there.

My increase in market share attracted a few raised eyebrows. I hadn't been seen as a significant player at Fenway, but now that I'd moved into shirts, my stock was rising, and Worm was complaining about me cutting into his sales. I sensed that the Bouncer was aware of the moves I had made and that I, too, would have to come to some arrangement with him as Worm had a few years before. Knowing the ask was coming soon, I offered the Bouncer a tribute out of respect (and to avoid any additional headaches), passing some money along after every home stand.

The Bouncer was familiar with what I was doing with Bridge Nine, and I wasn't shy in talking about how I was investing the money into the bands; by this time, I'd released more than forty new recordings, and many of the bands were local. There'd even been talk of my releasing a record for a band he was starting. We shared a mutual respect. I was swimming in cash, and the potential goodwill greatly outweighed the cost. Of course, every dollar added up by the end of the season, but compared to what we were making down there, it seemed like short money.

The Bouncer appreciated the gesture and clarified that while Worm got nothing in return for the money he paid, I could let him know if I needed help. While I didn't think it would come to that, I saw it as an insurance policy I would hopefully never use. Our team of vendors had dealt with everyone who had tried to compete with us, but if someone more serious challenged us at some point, I didn't think it wouldn't hurt to have someone with a vested interest to turn to for help.

CHAPTER 17

Witch City

IN EARLY 2003, HYDRA HEAD PICKED UP AND MOVED WEST TO join Big Wheel Recreation in Los Angeles. They vacated their second-floor office, and instead of giving it back to the landlord, I moved my quickly expanding Fenway operation in and absorbed their space. I even bought all their warehouse shelves, which went from holding their over-stock records to holding my T-shirts. The timing was great; whenever I was running out of space, someone in the office was leaving, giving me the necessary room to accommodate my growing enterprise. My catalog of slogan shirts was getting larger and included ones that proudly proclaimed, "Hey Yankees Fans, Yank This!" with an arrow pointing down to the wearer's groin and the equally ignorant (yet wildly popular) "Take Your 26 Rings and Shove 'Em Up Your Ass." Yankees fans *loved* to remind us of how many championship rings the team had earned over the years compared to Boston's five. I ordered those shirts by the pallet and flooded the streets with them. I bought a half-dozen black wire carts and filled them with shirts for our vendors to push to their selling locations each game. We were genuinely pandering to the lowest common denominator.

Shockingly loud and offensive T-shirts got a lot of laughs, and as people stopped and laughed, they spent money.

Now that I was selling shirts, working with and around the Codees became more of a priority. I made it clear that, while I respected they had a job to do, I would still try to circumvent them whenever possible. On a Saturday at the start of the summer, the Codees caught up with one of my daytime vendors, Kat—one of Bridge Nine's interns that moonlighted hawking shirts—and confiscated her entire inventory, cart and all. I was back at the Boylston Street office when I learned of the loss. My cell phone vibrated in the pocket of my jeans. I pulled it out and flipped it open.

"Chris! They took everything!" I could hear that she was crying. "All my shirts, the cart, they even took my permit," she sobbed.

Ahh, crap. This was a first. The days of outrunning the Codees when all you had was a courier bag around your shoulder were over; it's harder to escape with a hundred T-shirts crammed into a cart weighing you down.

"Don't worry; I'll figure something out," I replied. I hung up and called Tiger.

"Hey, Tiger! Did one of your guys just confiscate a cart from one of my vendors?"

"She's with you?" he replied. Word of her bust had made it to him. "I heard she didn't take it well."

"Yeah, she's new to this. I don't think she was ready for you guys."

"I'll see what I can do," he replied and hung up.

Thirty minutes later, Kat called me back. Dejected, she had walked back to her apartment in Mission Hill empty-handed. When she got home her cart, still filled with shirts, awaited her on the front steps. Lying on top was her hawker and peddler license, which had her address printed on it.

When Kat was approached and informed her cart was being impounded, she'd burst into tears. After the Codee had packed the cart into their car and driven away with her permit, either they'd changed their heart and returned the seized goods to her apartment instead of keeping them locked up, or Tiger had intervened and put in a good word for me. The game hadn't ended yet, and it was obvious she hadn't sold anything, so maybe they decided that the lost opportunity was punishment enough. Either way, it was appreciated and made it easier to convince Kat to return to sell at the next game.

At the Initech office, it was getting harder to move around. I'd filled the upstairs space I'd recently gained with sports T-shirts. Downstairs, I'd begun stacking boxes as high as possible in every available corner. Open space had been at a premium from the get-go, but I'd released dozens of new record titles since moving in and had reached the saturation point. Officemate Matt Pike had just become a dad the previous fall and was having trouble justifying the daily commute from his home in Salem, Massachusetts, so he asked that we consider looking for new office space on the North Shore. Salem had a few large industrial buildings with open spaces available. He'd spent a couple of years in one such building working for Rykodisc, an independent record label that had made a name for itself by being one of the first to license and release classic titles on CD by notable artists like Elvis Costello, Frank Zappa, and David Bowie, at a time when record labels saw the new format as a fad.

Our mutual friends at Deathwish, who had been operating from the basement of a house one town over in Beverly, were also looking for a new office. We were already collaborating quite a bit between our compilation-label samplers and sharing merch tables at a few different music festivals around the country. We agreed to join forces with a new North Shore space and replicate the cooperative spirit that had started in Boston's Fenway neighborhood. I kept the Initech space as a dedicated office for my street-vending business, and we split a more affordable (and significantly larger) space between Bridge Nine, Deathwish, and the Kenmore Booking Agency twenty miles north in Salem, more commonly known as the Witch City from its association with the witch trials of 1692. Elisabeth and I had been living in Boston for the past year, so I asked her if she was open to moving to Salem. It was an idea she warmed up to once she learned the ride on the commuter train to her job in Boston would be faster than her current trip from Mission Hill in a Green Line subway streetcar. We were both apprehensive about leaving Boston, but Salem, with its weird vibe, resonated with us. Elisabeth asked a friend already living there if she'd stand out as a heavily tattooed woman, to which he replied, "I saw a guy wearing a sword on his back yesterday. You'll be fine."

Bridge Nine wasn't just leaving Boston for more space; the label was also considering leaving Lumberjack as our distributor. There was talk of them ending their arrangement with Caroline for a new deal with Navarre Corporation, a distribution company better known for selling computer software than music. Caroline had a rich history with the kind of music I'd grown up with, releasing records on their label with hardcore bands like Bad Brains, Youth of Today, Misfits, Warzone, and Underdog, a few of my all-time favorites. It may have been naive then, but I didn't like Lumberjack's direction. It seemed to be too far separated from the community where we all started and more about how many zeroes the owner could get as a cash advance. In July 2003, we sent them a letter regarding our intention to leave. Lumberjack's value as a distributor was based on the catalog of labels it had under contract, and ours had renewed automatically months earlier for another year, so they advised they'd take legal action and make an example out of us if we left for Caroline. With all our money and resources tied into releasing records and no funds for litigation, we had to stay put.

We waited for the deal to expire, a time complicated by Lumberjack delaying payments to us and by the poaching of bands. Over a few months, we saw deals with Slapshot, Blood for Blood, Ramallah, and Madball disappear when the bands accepted last-minute higher offers with Toledo-based Thorp Records—deals underwritten by Lumberjack. Thorp was happy to collaborate with us when we did the *Fighting Music* compilations, but now they had someone else's money and some leverage. Despite all the headaches I faced, Lumberjack would end up going out of business just six years later, taking down scores of independent labels and offering the ones still standing only ten cents on the dollar of what they owed, so I felt lucky that I had gotten out while the getting was good. And Thorp? They folded a year after Lumberjack.

I had another mess to deal with that summer, when my concerns with Bridge Nine's employee Darren came to a head. Once word got out that he was working at Bridge Nine, a few people he'd allegedly wronged on some level came out of the woodwork to warn me about him. He'd initially come across as solid, but over the course of the year he'd been with me, I was starting to question if that was the case.

On Darren's own time, he'd offered to help get a CD manufactured for a friend who was releasing an album's worth of solo material by the Bouncer. Darren had given a lot of lip service, deadlines were repeatedly not met, and they were tired of waiting. Darren wasn't a Boston guy, so the memo regarding the Bouncer being on the short list of people in the city to never fuck around with hadn't made it to him. The Bouncer didn't want to hear excuses. Midmove to the new Salem office, we went to a mostly empty Initech space to survey what was left when my cell phone rang. It was the Bouncer.

"Hey, Chris, are you around?" he asked. "And is Darren with you?"

"Yeah, we're headed to the Boylston Street office," I replied. "We'll be there in about fifteen minutes." I thought it was odd that the Bouncer was calling me to look for Darren. The expression on Darren's face told me the Bouncer had tried calling him first, and he hadn't picked up.

Shortly after we returned to the nearly vacated space, the Bouncer and one of his friends walked down the front steps of the vestibule into the office and greeted us. Darren was led around the corner farther into the office so the Bouncer could speak with him while the friend started making small talk with the rest of us. I was suddenly aware of what was likely happening in the other room but could do nothing to stop it, even if I wanted to. Darren had brought this upon himself, and I was thankful not to be considered guilty by association.

The friend picked up my button handpress off a stack of remaining boxes destined for the new office and gently let it hang from his grip as he appreciated the heavy weight of its all-steel construction. One of my earliest investments, it allowed me to manufacture one-inch-diameter punk-rock buttons, which I'd made one at a time and sold for years off merch tables. It was about twenty inches tall with a hinge in the middle, so it swung by his side as he smiled. I looked at him and knew exactly what he was thinking, and as I slowly shook my head with a nervous laugh, I said, "Please, don't." I didn't want the roughly six-pound button maker used as a battle mace on Darren. He'd jerked around the wrong people and would have to answer for it, but that could have killed him. Thankfully, he gently placed it back on top of the box.

We could hear a commotion coming from inside the office, and Darren ended up in a ball on the floor as the Bouncer kicked him repeatedly. The Bouncer wasn't going to post a complaint about Darren's slow service on the internet; there would be no call to the Better Business Bureau. If you lied to this dude, you were simply getting laid out on the floor. His message sent, the two were gone as quickly as they'd arrived. Darren awkwardly got up off the ground and pulled himself together, picking up his glasses and adjusting them back on his face while straightening his shirt as he walked back over to us. Flustered but still in one piece, Darren said, "That's the sort of thing that can happen when you do business with people like that," as if getting beaten to the ground over repeatedly missing a delivery date was as common as overdraft bank fees or a customer stiffing you on an order.

I locked the office door, and we left, aware that Darren's price for jerking the Bouncer around could have been much worse. I was appalled that he took no accountability in the situation, even after getting his ass kicked. But in the middle of a move and desperate for any help I could get, I waited to fire him until a few days later. I should have done it months earlier, but I'd been too overwhelmed by the prospect of taking back the responsibilities he'd assumed. At this point, I had no choice; he was toxic and a threat to my business.

I'd later find out that Darren had used his position at the label to open up lines of credit with some of our vendors for his own purposes and racked up bills that he never paid, which caused a lot of stress when they started reaching out to me to try to collect. I also discovered he'd stolen collectible copies of Hydra Head's vinyl releases, only to be caught selling them on eBay. Darren had also helped design some album layouts for Bridge Nine, notably Terror's debut. It turns out he'd ripped off elements from American Nightmare's *The Sun Isn't Getting Any Brighter* EP that Jacob Bannon had designed and used them to create the texture of the *Lowest of the Low* album cover—a bush-league move that made me and Bridge Nine look bad.

With Darren gone, I spent the end of the summer of 2003 in Salem organizing our new cooperative space. Deathwish and Bridge Nine hired a shared employee to work for both labels, a guy who went by the name Jeff Jawk, who relocated from Atlanta to join us. He had started his own DIY record label in 1996 under the name Jawk Records, but his label was no longer active, so Jeff was seeking a new opportunity.

I pushed out a wave of new 7-inch singles to mail-order customers, which included two records by a new band called Stand & Fight featuring Wrench from Ten Yard Fight singing, along with Boston's up-and-comers Mental, Southern California's F-Minus, and a picture disc single for American Nightmare under their new name, Give Up the Ghost. They had chosen the new moniker after being sued by a bar rock band from Philadelphia that had been using the name American Nightmare a few years longer. Apparently, the Philly band's drummer worked in a law office and had successfully trademarked the name. The legal struggle that ensued almost broke up Boston's American Nightmare. It was an outrage, as the band from Philadelphia was basically a cover band that had never toured, while Tim and Wes were putting Boston hardcore on the worldwide stage.

Most amazingly, I was releasing a 7-inch with one of my favorite bands from before I'd started the label: Sick of It All. Seventeen-year-old me wouldn't have believed it. Twenty-seven-year-old me still couldn't. Their lyrics had inspired me to "scratch the surface" a decade earlier, and I was doing so with the intention of leaving a permanent mark.

By September, just as things were settling down, I boarded a flight to join Terror for their (and my) first tour in Japan. Five shows were booked over a week supporting the *Lowest of the Low* EP, which I had licensed to a label in Tokyo. The buzz around them was enormous; you could see and hear that they would be one of the biggest hardcore bands in the world. I went for the sole reason of being Bridge Nine's ambassador—I wanted to greet everyone as the face of the label and promote the brand, making it easier for more Bridge Nine bands to tour there as my bands continued to expand across the globe.

CHAPTER 18

The 2003 American League Championship Series

IN THE 2003 SEASON, THE RED SOX HAD A RECORD OF NINETY-five wins and sixty-seven losses, their most wins since 1986 when they had last earned a trip to the World Series, but they finished second behind the Yankees. Boston beat Oakland in the ALDS and headed to the Bronx for the first two games in New York, striking first and beating the Yankees 5–2. The Red Sox may have been playing two states away, but I was in Boston trying to keep up with the demand for T-shirts, selling them to fans around the park at all the bars.

I bought a few steel-framed garden utility carts with large rubber tires and a four-foot bed, secured two full-size garbage cans on top of each with bungee cords, and filled them full of shirts. Nicknamed "the Tanks," I had three teams of two walking up and down the streets around the empty stadium, posting up near entrances to popular bars, tossing free shirts to the doormen to let us linger and sell to their patrons. One person would lead with the cart, while the other walked alongside it and sold tees out of the garbage cans. Officer Tiger and his crew weren't around because games weren't being played in Boston, so we had free rein, and after that first game, we almost completely sold out of everything we'd brought.

The ALCS was Boston's first postseason matchup with the Yankees since 1999, when they'd lost 4–1 and had to watch the Yankees win it all after beating the Atlanta Braves in the World Series. The energy around the park for the first two games was electric; people crowded the sidewalks while Fenway Park stood quiet and dark. The eighteen-story "GO SOX" message spelled out in lights on the side of the Prudential Center loomed over the skyline in the distance. They were two of my best nights selling T-shirts, since we were hawking them for the entire length of the game and not just limited to the postgame rush. When Sox sluggers David Ortiz and Manny Ramirez launched home runs in the fourth and fifth innings of Game One, respectively, fans lost their minds inside the bars, and their cheers of "Yankees suck!" reverberated into the streets where we stood selling to the crowds of customers circling the Tanks. People were caught up in the excitement and didn't even care what they bought; they just wanted something in the moment. If we didn't have their size, they just went up or down one size or grabbed a different shirt. It was one of the only times I returned to the old Initech space with empty carts.

The Yankees took the second game, and the series returned to Boston split 1–1. Game Three was a highly anticipated matchup between starting pitchers Pedro Martínez for Boston and Roger Clemens for New York. This was their first postseason game going head-to-head since Game Three of the 1999 Championship Series, where Boston's only win in the series was a 13–1 trouncing the night before Ten Yard Fight's final performance. Clemens had announced his imminent retirement earlier in the season, and this would likely be his last game at Fenway. The Red Sox struck first when Manny Ramirez knocked a line drive into center field on the second pitch, scoring two runs in the first inning and electrifying the crowd. New York would respond, scoring once in the top of the second, once in the third, and twice in the fourth.

In the top of the fourth inning, Martínez hit a Yankee with a pitch. As retaliation, that player made a point to slide hard into the Sox infielder who was protecting second base. That was part of the tit-for-tat politics of baseball; you hit my guy, I'm hitting yours. Players yelled at each other, and warnings were issued. As the umpires got involved in keeping things from escalating, a loud "Yankees suck!" chant overtook the crowds.

At the bottom of the fourth, an errant pitch by Roger Clemens to Manny Ramirez was seen as further escalation. Ramirez began walking toward the mound and pointed at Roger, yelling at him. Immediately, the benches cleared, and both teams ran onto the field. Yankees bench coach Don Zimmer, who at seventy-two years of age had spent his entire adult life in baseball after signing with the Brooklyn Dodgers as an amateur free agent in 1949, also rushed the field, zeroing in on Pedro Martínez before being swiftly pushed by Pedro to the ground. Don had played baseball back when batters weren't required to wear helmets and in 1953 took a pitch to his head that put him in the hospital for two weeks, unconscious and needing holes drilled into his skull to relieve the pressure from swelling. So he clearly took personal exception to what he thought had been Martínez purposely throwing at his batter earlier in the inning.

As the dust settled, Don was escorted off the field to the echoing chants of "Yankees suck!" Beer sales were stopped inside the stadium to keep the crowds from getting even more unruly. No one on the field was ejected from the game, where the Yankees ultimately won 4–3. The rivalry's flames were stoked even higher, and Boston manager Grady Little was later quoted saying, "We've upgraded from a battle to a war." Red Sox fans were fired up, translating to another night of heavy-duty T-shirt sales. The following day, the *New York Post* tried to demonize Pedro by printing the headline "Fenway Punk" in large letters above a photo of him looming over a falling Don Zimmer.

After six games, the Red Sox and Yankees were even at three wins apiece, sending Boston back to New York for a dramatic Game Seven. This was do-or-die territory for the Sox and the shirt vendors, and leading up to the game was a shirt-selling frenzy. I wanted to make the most of the opportunity that excitement presented, so I drove Elisabeth's red Mustang to the Haymarket T station in downtown Boston with two Rubbermaid bins packed tightly with T-shirts to catch the crowds leaving after work. I was one block from city hall, trying to avoid being visible from the building. I didn't need a flashy, look-at-me display, just a spot with a lot of foot traffic. At this point, it was a numbers game; I knew the shirts would sell. I just needed enough people to pass by to ensure that I would move them all.

"Get your T-shirts he-ah!" I yelled, dropping my *r*'s and dragging the word out as I waved a "Cowboy Up" shirt. I also had a bin filled with two "Yankee Hater" designs, but the "Cowboy Up" phrase made popular by relief pitcher Mike Timlin and first baseman Kevin Millar was currently leading the pack in sales. "Cowboy Up" proved to be another gift from the T-shirt gods. The anti-Yankees classics were still selling well, but this was something new with a positive sentiment; it was a rallying cry for Boston to pick itself up and keep trying. I thought it was weird to be "going western" in New England, but it had become what people were looking for, as the phrase was posted everywhere. The city had even added it to their blinking construction signs on the highway. And most important, it was selling, so that's all I cared about. I started with five hundred of them and had to call for a reprint days later. It was transactional, like the stickers I'd sold to Hot Topic years before. Give the people what they want.

As quickly as I could grab a shirt from the bin, another person held cash out to me, and I flung the tee over another shoulder. That is, until I heard an even more authentic Boston accent loudly question, "What in the fuck do you think you're doing?" It was Mackie, a.k.a. Don Mackleton, a Codee with a deep disdain for the shirt vendors. Things had become personal for him.

The previous winter, he'd run into Rod and the Suckers outside of the Garden as he left a Bruins game. He had been drinking, was out with friends to watch the game, and was not acting in any official capacity. Still, in his drunken state, he took it upon himself to be confrontational and try to police the crew as they sold shirts to the crowds, leading to an argument where Mackie apparently put his hands on Rod. Not having any of it, Rod beat Mackie's ass into the sidewalk—at least that was how it was later described to me with great enthusiasm and detail by the guys who saw it happen first-hand. Mackie reported the assault to his Codee supervisor and demanded action. Sadly for him, an internal investigation determined it to be a valid ass whooping as he was off the clock and should have never approached Rod in the first place.

That kind of thing would be hard to put behind you, so it was understandable that he would continue to flex on us when given a chance. He stood and smiled because he knew he had me dead to rights and there was nowhere I could go. My bins of T-shirts were loaded into the back of his patrol car, and he handed me a pink "embargoed property report" sheet detailing the 143 T-shirts he'd seized. He also gave me a bright-orange citation for making unauthorized sales, earning me a $200 fine, my second in the past two days. It was four in the afternoon, and I had gambled and lost. The big payoff would be at Fenway later that night, but I hadn't been able to resist the pregame sales downtown, and now a chunk of inventory was locked in the back of a Codee car. I wasn't stressed, though, because I had more than $1,000 in cash in my pocket and had to walk pre-game about a hundred yards into city hall to pay the fine. I was back at Mackie's car in twenty minutes, and, upon seeing the "Paid in Full" stamp on the ticket he'd given me only moments earlier, I could retrieve my shirts and prepare to return to Fenway later that evening.

Game Seven was thrilling. Boston scored early and often, putting four runs on the board halfway through the game. We were looking good at 4–0.

Was this actually the year? The first time the Red Sox would beat the Yankees in the postseason on their way to a World Series? Game Seven was a rematch of Game Three, pitting Pedro Martínez against Roger Clemens one last time. Sox fans were on top of the world, and, by the sixth inning, with Boston still up 4–1, they were already budgeting to see if they could afford tickets for Game One of the World Series, which would start the following Saturday at Fenway Park, should the Sox prevail. The Yankees earned a run in the bottom of the 7th, and David Ortiz homered in the top of the 8th to maintain Boston's three-run lead, but despite Martínez's early dominance, manager Grady Little famously kept him in the game too long. By the end of the eighth inning, Martínez had given up three more runs, tying the game to the dread of Sox fans.

All attention was focused on the game at the bars around Fenway Park, and the celebratory atmosphere was dampened as Red Sox fans watched the game go into extra innings. Finally, in the bottom of the eleventh, pitcher Tim Wakefield who'd started Games One and Four in the series, was brought in to stop the bleeding Pedro had allowed and saw his first pitch get drilled by Yankees infielder Aaron Boone. The ball was launched deep into left field, earning the Yankees a trip to their thirty-ninth World Series. It was instant heartbreak for Boston fans but a cold, empty, yet familiar feeling they'd long become accustomed to.

As the Yankees celebrated on the field in New York, Red Sox fans who'd been watching the game in Boston's bars lowered their heads and walked out in single-file lines. No emotions were expressed, just shell-shocked fans who walked away in an eerily quiet trance. The Curse of the Bambino had struck again, and with one crack of a bat, the money we had been showering in ceased to rain down upon us. After making our final sales, we returned to the office to retire the carts, the Red Sox season now over.

CHAPTER 19

Sully's

FRIDAY, OCTOBER 17, 2003. WHEN THE FOURTH SEASON OF vending outside Fenway ended, taking with it any chance of making more money, I had to find other ways to keep the cash flowing. I'd become accustomed to earning from April through September, but the label had grown exponentially, so I could no longer wait six months for another big infusion of funds. With baseball covered, I tried branching into hockey, basketball, and football. Fans of the first two sports congregated at the Garden, a downtown-Boston arena just three miles from Fenway Park, right in the middle of Boston's North End, Beacon Hill, and West End neighborhoods. The Red Sox played eighty-one regular-season home games at Fenway, but collectively the Bruins and Celtics played eighty-two. The capacity of the Garden was half that of Fenway Park, but there was an opportunity there.

I didn't know the first thing about hockey other than it was played on ice; I hadn't grown up around the sport outside of attending the occasional Hartford Whalers game as a kid. But I went with what I knew: Bruins fans drank a lot of beer, and hockey players regularly dropped their gloves and fought it out on the ice. So "Drink Beer and Fight" became my first slogan offered. The design incorporated athletic gold lettering over hockey sticks on a black tee. Throughout the season, the shirt steadily became the focal piece in the uniform worn proudly by thousands of Bruins fans.

Selling at the Garden turned street vending into a yearlong hustle. The Garden was a different animal from Fenway, though. There were only two entrances to cover, so we didn't need as large of a crew. The facility had security guards in all-black military-fatigue uniforms who would actively keep vendors off their section of sidewalk, but the federal building that abutted the Garden's property had an elevated walkway that ran alongside the entrance sidewalk leading into the arena. The walkway had a row of large, decorative granite pyramids running along it, which made an excellent surface for displaying shirts to the crowds as they left after the game. We could post up within thirty feet of the Garden's entrance and not physically be on their property. As people left, they'd wander up to us, and we'd make sales over the handrail that separated the properties. The walkway was also covered, so it helped keep us dry during inclement weather, something we couldn't avoid at Fenway.

At that time, Causeway Street was still running under the elevated Green Line tracks, so there was only a narrow staircase leading up to it. That ensured that one of the best spots to sell was standing on the concrete jersey barriers next to the T station entrance, where crowds of hundreds of people at a time had to wait their turn to walk up the stairs in a single-file line. The hardest part of catching customers at Fenway was when they walked swiftly past you; here, we had a captive audience staring at our gear for upwards of ten minutes, giving us plenty of time to make a sale.

Before us, the shirts for sale on the street were primarily counterfeits: T-shirts made to look like officially licensed Red Sox or Bruins shirts by featuring the team's actual logos, but bootlegged and offered at a discounted price. We took a different approach, using popular slogans in the public domain that resonated with fans. Not protected by a trademark, *Boiling*

Point fanzine-inspired "Yankees Suck" shirts had proliferated, available in every souvenir store and gas station and sold online from a hundred different vendors. While existing in that space kept us from the grasp of the league's lawyers, our ideas were also firmly within reach of every other sports fan in Boston with access to a screen-printing press.

For this reason, I began to see the value of creating my own intellectual property. The Sucks Guys had been arrested outside of the Garden over their "Celtic Pride" T-shirts, which had stepped too closely onto the Celtics' toes. They were subjected to a full-on police-van raid where everyone was taken in on fluffed-up counterfeit charges. Those were later dropped, but the Suckers had to stop selling the shirt. The team should have just cut the Suckers a check for the idea because shortly after, a fancier version of their Celtic Pride design popped up in the official team store.

Not looking to get caught up in the same drama, I paired a white shamrock on a kelly-green tee but featured a new slogan: "Believe in Boston." Hawking "Celtic Pride" shirts had gotten Rod and the Suckers arrested, and I'd learned "Boston Pride" was a commodity anyone could make—whoever offered the cheapest option got the sale. But "Believe in Boston" didn't exist in the marketplace. If I could market something unique that people wanted and could adequately protect it—starting with registering a state trademark—I could prevent other people from using the phrase, gaining value and leverage over my competitors.

I had spent most of the first four years exclusively hating on the Yankees, with few exceptions. Developing merchandise that said "Believe in Boston" was an opportunity to break from that cycle of negativity and focus on the positive, rooting *for* something instead of against. Smack-talking rivals was getting old and making us look bitter, and I wanted to be known as the guy who repped Boston more than the guy who shit-talked New York. I also realized I needed more than just a slogan. My street-vending operation needed a name, one that personified Boston without pigeonholing itself. I chose the name Sully's. It was relatable; everyone in New England knew someone with the nickname Sully. It evoked Boston but wasn't tied to a single sport. It was also what we'd been calling some of the most belligerent fans, saying we'd been hassled "by a couple of Sullys" when dodging the drunk and disorderly, a nightly occurrence. Since we were in the business of making belligerent T-shirts, the name fitted.

I had been directing my online customers to a website called YankeeHater.com, and it wasn't the best place to promote shirts catering to Celtics and Bruins fans, despite the mutual feelings. I explored bringing "Yankee Hater" nationwide, initially offering different colorways for fans of teams that were also rivals of the Yankees. Ultimately, however, I decided to focus on just Boston and worked to tie everything under the Sully's brand name. In November 2003, I started a website for Sully's and made it a year-round business.

At first, branding my shirts with the name Sully's was just a way to separate us from the other shirt hawkers. Beyond our shirts having arguably more clever slogans and designs than the competition, there hadn't been much of an effort to differentiate ourselves from the other people slinging tees, like the two knuckleheads who sold T-shirts out of a suitcase or the hippie guy who drove from Sturbridge, fifty miles away, to sell his shirts like he was tailgating in the parking lot of a Grateful Dead concert.

It dawned on me that I had two businesses, and the one I started by accident was doing much better than the one I began on purpose. The label was burning through money getting new albums recorded and pressed, and anything earned just went back into the pot to help underwrite the next batch of records. Sully's, on the other hand, was overcome with opportunity. If I made a T-shirt for a band, I would sell dozens of them. If I made a T-shirt talking shit about someone on the Yankees, I sold thousands of them. The money was covering my rent and living expenses. It also paid off my college loans and funded everything I was trying to accomplish with

Bridge Nine while reinvesting the rest into Sully's to help the brand meet its potential.

The push into other opportunities for Sully's was primarily due to the lack of money from Bridge Nine's distributor, Lumberjack. With the label's cash flow cut off from retail sales as we waited out the end of our Lumberjack contract, I had to depend more on our direct mail-order sales and anything I could pull together via sports fans through Sully's. So I started throwing whatever I could on a T-shirt if I thought it could sell and fielded suggestions for shirt ideas that would appeal to Bruins and Celtics fans from friends in bands who were bigger sports fans than I was.

In December, I sat down with the print shop's owner to pay bills from the previous month. In the past two years, I'd gone from ordering shirts by the dozens to the hundreds and into the thousands at a time. I'd become their biggest customer, a status confirmed as she gushed about how great it was that we were doing such big numbers. It was a good shop, and it had been convenient to work with them, but my independent need to DIY had already begun to take over. It would be much cheaper to start printing my shirts in-house. The print shop was great about pushing orders through, but they kept dinging me with rush fees on the quick turnarounds I needed. If Sully's became vertically integrated and started printing the shirts ourselves, we could likely capitalize on opportunities faster by controlling production. To that end, I considered starting my own screen-printing business—which was crazy, as I had zero experience with screen printing outside of being a weekly screen-printing customer. I also needed $20,000 to get it off the ground. That didn't deter me.

I already knew what I was going to call it: Liberated Images, a name I'd first used in college as the title of my final art exhibit. I later resurrected it in Boston to help market products I designed that weren't necessarily music or sports related. I recruited two of Jeff Jawk's friends from Atlanta who had printing experience and were looking to move out of the South. They got to work right away building out a printing space. The tenant next to Bridge Nine in the new Salem office building had moved out, so we took over their lease and added a doorway between the spaces. It would be many months before the first shirt would come off our press, but I was taking steps in the right direction.

The new year kicked off with another Patriots Super Bowl win, and Boston fans rioted as part of the celebration, flipping cars and even setting a few of them on fire. A twenty-one-year-old visiting his brother at Northeastern was killed when he and several others were run over by an SUV trying to escape the unruliness. The previous fall's Red Sox loss in Game Seven to the Yankees still hurt, but one of our first T-shirts of 2004 simply stated hopefully, "This Is Our Year," perhaps in an effort to manifest a winning season. Liberated Images started printing our simplest T-shirts in our Salem warehouse by June, so we made anything with one color of ink on a white T-shirt while we continued to farm out our more complex two- and three-color designs.

Salem was beginning to feel like a home for Elisabeth and me. In a few short years, I'd gone from running around the neighborhood in Boston getting in fights to trying to manage multiple growing businesses, and she brought stability into our relationship. I don't know if I would have made it out of Mission Hill in one piece if not for her, to be honest. She was the voice of reason many times. I was a risk-taker, while she was extremely cautious. We balanced each other in many ways, so we moved out of our rented apartment and bought a condo, putting down more permanent roots. I asked her to marry me on the evening of her birthday that summer, and she said yes.

Meanwhile, Terror opted to leave the label after they'd initially agreed to do their first full-length album with me, largely because of the trouble Bridge Nine had keeping their CD in stock. It was additional fallout from Darren not doing his job and giving the band and me the same lip service he'd given the Bouncer, but he was long gone by the time the damage was done. Terror offered to let us press the vinyl for the album as an olive branch, while the more profitable CD and digital sales went to another label.

After a combination of factors that included the stress of the legal challenge to the band's name, an emotionally exhausted Wes decided to break up American Nightmare/Give Up the Ghost on the eve of a European tour, effectively ending an era they had dominated. A newly formed band of young hardcore-punk fans from New Bedford, Have Heart, was building hype in the Boston area and was on a similar trajectory as American Nightmare had been a few years earlier. While American Nightmare had kept their T-shirts almost exclusively black, Have Heart had grown tired of that look and wanted to inject color into the crowd at shows. Their first EP was being released on a label run by a member of the band Outbreak, for whom I was about to press a record, and several members of Have Heart soon joined us as hawkers outside of Fenway Park. Once again, the music scene was beginning to shift. Things were about to change in a big way for the Red Sox too.

CHAPTER 20

Concessions

ONE OF THE RED SOX'S WEAPONS FOR THE 2004 SEASON WAS starting pitcher Curt Schilling, who had come to Boston from Arizona. To celebrate his arrival, I designed a T-shirt with the phrase "Killin' with Schillin'" around the silhouette of a .38 Special on the front, riffing on the number 38 on his jersey and drawing the parallel of a pitcher to a firearm. It was probably in poor taste to have an illustration of a gun on a shirt, especially after Rod had been shot in our apartment years earlier, but I sold more than two thousand of them before Opening Day—many to fans at the Garden headed home after Celtics and Bruins games—and their popularity continued after the season started, especially after actor Ben Affleck was pictured wearing one in *People* magazine. A hot seller outside Fenway Park, the shirt also attracted the attention of easily offended, pearl-clutching fans bothered by the gun reference, and they set in motion a campaign to rid the streets of it. Within days, enough complaints about the shirt had made it to city hall that Boston mayor Thomas Menino himself dispatched Tiger to address it. He caught up with me after a rough loss to the Cleveland Indians.

"Hey, Chris," he said. "I got a call from the mayor over your Schilling shirt."

"Oh, yeah? Does he want one? What's his size?" I jokingly replied.

"Ha!" Tiger laughed. "Not exactly . . . he wants it off the street. There's been a spike in gun violence and murders in Boston, and having a shirt sold with a gun on it out on a city street isn't a good look. I did tell him you would have a First Amendment defense to keep selling it, though."

Damn, I thought.

"Tell him to consider it gone then," I responded.

"Yeah?" Tiger asked, surprised.

"Sure." The shirt had been a success, but it was just one of many. I could concede one design to keep the friggin' mayor of Boston off my back. It was selling well online and in a few stores, so it wasn't like I'd be stuck with them.

"I'll let him know. Thank you," Tiger responded.

I returned to the print shop to pick up another order of my second recent bestseller, "A-Rod Is an A-Hole." Aaron Boone, who'd robbed Boston of their postseason hopes in 2003, tore a ligament in an offseason pickup basketball game, so the Yankees traded for Texas Rangers infielder Alex "A-Rod" Rodriguez to fill his spot at third base. A-Rod was the American League Most Valuable Player the previous year. His arrival in New York insulted all Red Sox fans, who'd anticipated his coming to Boston before a deal was nixed by the Players Association, paving the way for the Yankees' deal. He was the highest-paid athlete with the most lucrative sports contract: $252 million spread over ten years, and the Texas Rangers were looking to shed some of that payroll so they could rebuild by investing in younger players. At the time, I didn't realize how much A-Rod had wanted to become a member of the Red Sox, but with him heading to New York, the gloves were off. Early printings had quickly sold out, so I ordered a thousand more. I needed a dolly to load four boxes, about a third of the order, and push them back to the office. There they would be rolled tightly with a rubber band and stacked in bins, ready to be loaded into our selling carts. I just hoped A-Rod didn't have any relatives at Boston's city hall.

Heckling your team's rival was nothing new; and a hundred years earlier, Boston's most enthusiastic fans comprised a group called the Royal Rooters. They sang well-known songs of the day and substituted the lyrics with insults directed at the other team's players as they stood on the field. The chairman of the Rooters was none other than future mayor of Boston John "Honey Fitz" Fitzgerald, the maternal grandfather of John Fitzgerald Kennedy, the thirty-fifth president of the United States. Back then, the Rooters would stretch along the third baseline and repeatedly belt out these updated Broadway tunes in unison. Their most popular number was a song called "Tessie," and during the 1903 World Series between the Red Sox and Pittsburgh Pirates, they changed the lyrics from:

Tessie, you make me feel so badly.
Why don't you turn around?
Tessie, you know I love you madly.
Babe, my heart weighs about a pound.

to:

Honus, why do you hit so badly?
Take a back seat and sit down
Honus, at bat you look so sadly.
Hey, why don't you get out of town?

The updated lyrics targeted Pirates all-star shortstop (and future Hall of Famer) Honus Wagner. The story goes that the singing distracted Wagner and the Pirates so much that Boston went on to win what was the first World Series championship in 1903. The Royal Rooters remained organized in Boston until 1918, and the Red Sox won five titles under their watch. After the Rooters disbanded, the winning of championships ceased. Coincidence?

The sting of 2003's loss was still painful for the new Red Sox ownership, so they thought of outside-the-box ways to build morale during the 2004 season. Aware of the century-old song "Tessie" and the legend of how it helped the Red Sox win during those early years, the team's executive vice president of public affairs, Dr. Charles Steinberg, approached the Dropkick Murphys to request they record a contemporary version. After some initial reservations (the song itself needed serious updating), the band obliged, and, as part of the song's rollout, they performed it in late July when the Yankees were in town from a small stage on the warning track in Fenway Park's outfield in yet another ceremonial effort to "reverse" the Curse.

By this point in the season, the Red Sox were eight and a half games behind in the standings, and the fans' appetite for what we were selling had grown as the Yankees added to their lead over Boston. A-Rod received the brunt of Red Sox Nation's wrath. There were plenty of reasons for Boston fans to hate A-Rod, but it was more than sour grapes. A-Rod fitted in as a Yankee because he had their trademark smugness down, with a face that any Boston fan would love to take a swing at.

Two and a half innings after the Dropkicks Murphys performed, the Red Sox were already losing to the Yankees 3–0. Starting pitcher Bronson Arroyo was on the mound, and A-Rod was at the plate. Two outs, one strike, and one ball were on the board when Bronson's next pitch went a little inside, hitting A-Rod on the back of his elbow. As Rodriguez began to walk away from the batter's box, he angrily shouted at Bronson, "Throw that shit over the fucking plate!" Red Sox catcher Jason Varitek stood up and got between A-Rod and Arroyo; his job included protecting his starting pitcher. Varitek, more commonly referred to as V-Tek, reportedly replied, "We don't throw at .260 hitters," an insult referencing A-Rod's low batting average. That angered A-Rod, and it was on. V-Tek shoved his large leather catcher's mitt in A-Rod's face, providing a photo op that graced the cover of the *Boston Globe* newspaper the following day as the benches cleared and every member of both teams flooded the field. V-Tek was a formidable player who took his role in protecting his pitcher seriously. There was a reason I'd started selling "V-Tek Is a Beast" T-shirts a couple of months earlier; he didn't take any shit.

Red-and-white-uniformed players wrestled those with gray-and-navy uniforms as Varitek and A-Rod were engulfed by members of both teams and disappeared beneath the fray in what would be commemorated as one of the most memorable "battles" in the rivalry between the Red Sox and Yankees. And the cherry on top? The entire Red Sox team rushed the field once more that day—not to fight but rather to celebrate as a walk-off home run drove in the winning runs by third baseman Bill Mueller, putting Boston back on top, 11–10. This feat was made even more impressive because the Yankees' most effective closing pitcher, Mariano Rivera, had been on the mound. We sold every "A-Rod Is an A-Hole" T-shirt we brought out that night.

The next day my cell phone rang.

"Hey, it's Tiger." An unnecessary greeting; I'd recognize that Boston accent anywhere.

"What's up?" I asked.

"The mayor wanted me to thank you for pulling the Schilling shirt and told me to return the favor," Tiger responded. "So, if you can push your first guy back to the corner of the Bank of America parking lot, we won't make you move."

After he hung up, I stared at my cell phone and smiled. The 2004 season was shaping up nicely.

CHAPTER 21

Competition

BY 2004, THERE WERE FEWER AND FEWER MEMBERS OF THE vendor class of 2000 in our crew of hawkers. Rod left Boston and was back in upstate New York. Worm headed overseas once again, and the last anyone had heard, he was in Spain. Or was it Baghdad? Either way, I hadn't seen him around in months. Jesse Standhard handled the game-to-game operations for the Suckers. Jesse and I managed to keep competing newcomers behind us and to drive the point home that it was our show. I started bringing a couple of lawn chairs down to Kenmore Square for us to sit in, kicking back and lounging in front of the Bank of America as we oversaw our empire. Night after night, we chilled together and shot the shit, watching the crowds lumber by while our respective crews hustled tees in front of us and in full view of the competition that had to sell T-shirts deeper in Kenmore Square.

It became an established operation by that point. The land grab Jesse and I had to fight for together over the previous years resulted in defined borders. The Codees let us keep the first spot at the entrance of Kenmore Square, and we held that front line firmly. We were tasked with directing newcomers deeper into the area behind us; it was no longer a free-for-all. Still, the open block of sidewalk ahead of us continued to attract the interest of new T-shirt vendors who were unaware of the negotiations that had preceded their arrival.

Every few home stands, someone new would show up with their duffel bag of T-shirts looking to stake their claim. The sidewalk was starting to look like a T-shirt bazaar, with fifteen people peddling products out of bags and carts behind us on the way to the Green Line station entrance. We realized by this time that we didn't need to muscle people out; we just needed to let them know how the Codees had pushed everyone back and that they were welcome to set up behind us, which they always did. None of these new people selling shirts were particularly street-savvy. But, just as I had done years earlier, they gave it a shot. The difference was that they hadn't arrived with a dozen friends to back them up, so they took the path of least resistance, walking another fifty yards behind us when challenged.

That pattern held until two brothers from the North End, Boston's Italian enclave on the other side of Interstate 93, showed up with their own derivative "Yankees Suck" shirt. Nicknamed the "I-Ties" by our crew, I learned that they had a T-shirt kiosk in a park on Hanover Street and had decided to try to accommodate the potentially greater demand Fenway Park could warrant, putting them right in front of us at the edge of Kenmore Square. These guys were seasoned hustlers, ten to fifteen years older than us. When we approached them, they told us to fuck off. They weren't going anywhere. It was reminiscent of our first interactions with the 21-ers, just with the roles reversed. They offered a watered-down version of the Suckers' tee, and while Jesse's hawkers could have probably just worn them down with their bolder original, it was creating enough of a problem that talks about what to do turned to bringing in some outside help. Our crew would have run them out by force a few years earlier. The current vendors hadn't fought to maintain what they had, and by then, we had ironed out most of the headaches with the Codees, so I was the one who had to address issues as they popped up.

When I first started hawking in the street, I had nothing to lose; I was just a guy who owned nothing with a bunch of roommates who liked to fight. I now had an office filled with new albums, a mortgage, and a fiancée. If I could avoid it, I wouldn't be the one getting in people's faces anymore.

I mentioned the situation to the Bouncer one evening after the North End guys first became an issue, not looking for him to become involved but more to give him the lowdown of what had been happening. The I-Ties presented a hassle, but it was more the Sucks Guys' fight since it was their shirt that was getting knocked off. The Bouncer offered to help address it, but I downplayed the issue and told him I'd let him know how things were going; I didn't want him in the middle if I could avoid it.

It soon became clear that these guys weren't going away and had the means to dig in. On a phone call with the Bouncer days later, he again asked if I needed his help. It shouldn't have been my call, but none of the Suckers was willing to step up.

"If you want me to help you with this, you need to *tell* me that you want me to help you," he said meaningfully.

I hesitated. Deep down, I knew involving him would escalate the situation significantly. Still, I replied, "Yes," setting in motion events that could have had seriously dire consequences for all of us.

It was a warm evening in July, and we had just started setting up our carts. I stood on the sidewalk with two of the Suckers opposite me. In most areas, we'd post up near each other, and fans would walk between us; it was the most diplomatic way of competing among friends, letting the customer decide what they wanted to buy. We never poached each other's sales. Regarding anyone else behind us, we'd talk all sorts of shit—how the ink faded when you washed them or how the sleeves would fall off. The North End brothers set up near the street corner closest to the bridge, a good fifty feet in front of our first line, as they had in previous nights. The game was still going inside Fenway and the activity on the sidewalk was minimal, with few people coming and going. The Bouncer, wearing a sweatshirt with a hood pulled tightly over his head, approached one of the brothers and spoke with him. Their brief conversation ended abruptly as a cracking sound punctuated the air. The Bouncer had followed through with a brass knuckle–laden fist; talking had not proved productive, and violence was the final negotiating tool. As quickly as he'd arrived, the Bouncer disappeared. Tiger walked up from Kenmore Square moments later to find the injured I-Tie holding his face and asked him what had happened. Pulling his hand away to show his now bleeding and swelling eye, the I-Tie coldly replied, "You might want to take the next couple of nights off."

We were on high alert but couldn't afford to lay low. Friends of the Bouncer from within the punk scene traveled from as far as Philly to hang out around us the following weekend in case of retaliation, but things stayed quiet. A few weeks passed, and one evening as I was out on Newbury Street Extension, the street that ran behind Kenmore Square alongside the Mass Pike, I chatted with Tiger and another Codee as we waited for the game to close out. He mentioned seeing several people who looked out of place as he walked around. Kenmore Square had a predictable crowd on an average game night: the usual street vendors getting into position, the same few unhoused individuals asking for change outside of the 7-Eleven, and maybe a person or two waiting to use the ATM inside the bank lobby. Other than that, there weren't a lot of reasons to just be hanging out, but on this particular night, there seemed to be more than a few people who looked like they were waiting for something, and it stuck out to him. Tiger loved a good conversation; he'd chat anyone up, and it's part of what broke the ice between us early on. That night, he had casually said, "How's it going?" to someone he noticed posted in the square. The guy replied, "What do you care?" to which Tiger responded, "Just being friendly." The man retorted, "I hear it's not a friendly place."

As Tiger and I stood in the middle of the Newbury Street Extension, I noticed movement from behind a parked car at the meters overlooking the Mass Pike. Something didn't feel right, and I commented that I thought someone was creeping up on us. Tiger also sensed something was up, so he walked back into Kenmore Square while I crossed the bridge, thinking about what I'd seen. This should have sounded all sorts of alarms, but no one else had returned in the weeks after getting run out, so we naively continued.

An hour later, as my crew of vendors rolled their carts up from the office and headed toward Kenmore on the quiet stretch of road behind where the Rat nightclub had once stood, a dozen or more people rushed at us from the shadows. It was like a scene from the film *The Warriors* but set outside Fenway Park. The brothers from the North End had waited until they thought we'd least expect it and had brought an army of low-level thugs from their neighborhood, brandishing bats and pipes; one guy even carried a sword. The shirt vendors scattered and ran, leaving carts in the street to be impounded by the Codees.

While overwhelming, this show of force thankfully resulted in no serious injuries, with just a few of the guys going home bruised. That included a typically animated vendor named Noah, a friend of Max Powers who lived in Boston's West End. He didn't know the people who jumped us, but in Boston, it was surprisingly easy to connect the dots. Noah lived with his father, Duane, who had co-owned the Gallery East art space in Boston from 1979 until 1983. The Gallery East was an avant-garde gallery known as one of the city's earliest venues to hold all-ages hardcore-punk shows. Back then bars and nightclubs catered mainly to cover bands. If you wanted to play your own music, and especially if you were a punk band, you needed to find a nontraditional venue to perform in. The Gallery East was one such spot, and SS Decontrol and the Freeze christened their stage by performing there in August 1981. DYS, Negative Approach, the Meatmen, TSOL, Necros, and even Minor Threat had also played gigs there, earning it a secondary nickname, "home of the skinheads." Promotional flyers for shows at the Gallery East were reprinted years later in the book *Fucked Up + Photocopied*, putting the long-forgotten venue on the radar of the generation of hardcore-punk fans I was a part of.

Duane asked Noah what had happened to him. Noah was a tough kid who'd been raised practicing martial arts, and while he hadn't been injured, he had gotten scuffed up and had his shirt torn. Noah remarked that we'd been jumped over a shirt beef by guys from the North End, an area his father knew very well, having grown up there and operated a dojo teaching karate years earlier in the neighborhood. The following day, Duane walked Noah to his car and drove to Salem Street, one of the busier areas in the North End, where he saw a guy he knew was well connected in the area who could help him get to the bottom of things. Noah recounted the events of the previous evening, and they continued one block over to Hanover Street, home to some of Boston's best Italian restaurants and the heart of the city's oldest residential community.

The man brought Noah and Duane straight to a T-shirt cart on the Paul Revere Mall; he'd known the families of both parties for years and introduced Noah to the brothers. Once it was established that they had been behind the siege, he pointed to Noah and said, "He is one of us. You could have killed him. This ends today." The brothers were just as surprised as anyone to know how closely we were all connected, one of them having lived across the street from Duane's dojo years earlier. They were angry but agreed to back off, provided they had a chance to speak with me first, as I was seen as the head of the shirt crew and had been the first to approach them.

Duane called to update me—his involvement seemingly singlehandedly stopped what could have been a runaway train—and I will always be grateful for that. I agreed to meet with him and the brothers at the Prado, the open mall where they operated one of their T-shirt carts in the shadow of the Old North Church, the landmark made famous by Paul Revere's 1775 request to Boston patriots to hang lanterns there warning of British troop movements by saying, "One if by land, two if by sea."

The meeting time was set for noon as if it was the Old West, but instead of facing off with revolvers, the plan was for us to look each other in the eye and quash this feud face-to-face. The streets were filled with cars and delivery trucks, and the neighborhood buzzed as I walked toward the mall with Duane. He'd assured me everything was cool and I would walk out of this in one piece, but it still felt like I was being led into the lion's den. The brothers stood there waiting for us as we approached.

The reintroductions were brief and pleasantries minimal. They'd walked into Fenway and tried to knock off someone else's hustle, so what had ultimately gone down surprised nobody. The following escalation also benefited nobody, but as with most confrontations, neither party had been willing to back down. They knew they'd stepped on toes but also understandably didn't give a shit, much as we hadn't when we first arrived at Fenway Park, continuing the cycle. We had the opportunity to end it, and we did. The North End brothers didn't return to Fenway after that. Having immediately taken action to get us all to the table, Duane undoubtedly kept someone from getting hurt even worse.

For me, though, the consequences of the Bouncer tangling with the guys in the North End continued to unfold after he reassessed his liability. The arms race between camps after he became involved had significantly increased his risk, so the tribute I'd been passing along to him just in case this exact scenario happened was now required and would no longer be voluntary. If not for the lucky coincidence that we all knew and respected Duane, things could have gone very badly, very quickly.

To make the additional risk worthwhile and to address the inconvenience of his not being able to take his girlfriend out to dinner in the North End for the foreseeable future, the Bouncer informed me that I now needed to help him underwrite the short independent film he'd been working on.

He'd been using the money he was taking from Worm to finance it, but I had to come up with $2,500 to get him to his next goal. While the whole situation sucked and had been stressful for everyone involved, I'd made my own bed and had to deal with it. The Bouncer's filmmaking planted another cultural seed, and once again, the Fenway Park hustle was funding a punk's larger endeavors.

CHAPTER 22

Death Before Dishonor

TUESDAY, AUGUST 31, 2004. IF YOU'RE SUPERSTITIOUS, YOU may believe this was the day the "Curse of the Bambino" began to break, in the form of a teenage Red Sox fan's *teeth*. It wasn't the result of an erratic fist being swung in the mosh pit during a performance of Death Before Dishonor, the relatively new band I had announced as Bridge Nine's most recent signing earlier that day. Teeth had undoubtedly been inadvertently broken during their shows in the Boston area, but this tooth-bashing happened in the grandstands at Fenway Park. The Red Sox were four games behind the Yankees and had started a three-game series against the Anaheim Angels at Fenway. The Yankees were hosting the Cleveland Indians at home for two games. And sixteen-year-old Sox fan Lee Gavin was left holding his bloody mouth, two of his teeth knocked out, after a foul ball hit by his favorite player, Manny Ramirez, slammed through his outstretched hands into his face. Manny Ramirez blasting home run–distance balls wasn't news at Fenway; he led the team in homers during the 2004 season and had already hit two home runs earlier in the game, passing Red Sox great Jim Rice's career record of 382 by the time he sliced one into the stands just outside of the distinctive yellow "Pesky Pole" in right field, which was nicknamed in honor of Johnny Pesky, an old-timer who'd played for the Red Sox in the 1940s and '50s.

Lee may have been one of the thousands of teenage fans at Fenway that night, but he was the only one who lived in a home once owned by Babe Ruth. In the early 1920s, Ruth resided at the sprawling Sudbury farmhouse property during the offseason to appease his wife. It was an escape from the hard-partying lifestyle of a major leaguer in New York City and gave him a place where he could focus on getting into better shape. He'd gained quite a bit of weight, which appeared to have negatively affected his performance on the field. Ruth spent a couple of winters there before retreating to New York full-time, ultimately transferring the farmhouse to his wife as part of their separation. More than eight decades later, it had become Lee's family home. Evidence of Ruth's time there was etched into the living room's wooden floor in the form of burn marks where the ashes from his cigars fell and included regular visits from baseball fans who would pull up to the house to snap photos.

Manny's foul sent Lee Gavin to the hospital while he held his teeth—gathered by him and his friends—as well as the bloody ball, which had been retrieved and passed to him as security escorted him out.

But that foul ball wasn't the only shock of the night. Much to the delight of Red Sox fans, the tally of the Yankees-Indians game was being broadcast on Fenway's jumbotron scoreboard. The crowd delighted as the Indians scored three runs in each of the first three innings, going into the fifth inning in the Bronx with the Yankees down 9–0. The Indians scored six more times in the top of the fifth inning and handed the Yankees their most lopsided loss in franchise history, a stunning 22–0 collapse.

The Red Sox beat the Angels 10–7, shrinking the gap in the standings with the Yankees to three and a half games. The Sox victory at Fenway was sweet, but the Yankees' defeat in Cleveland was manna from heaven, inspiring me to design a commemorative T-shirt of New York's "22–0" loss. A local radio station became aware of the shirt, and, thanks to their multiple mentions of it on air, I sold more than five hundred of them, putting an extra $4,000 into our bank account over the next week as Red Sox fans wanting to relish the historic loss snapped up the shirts as a souvenir.

While I made the most of every opportunity to earn money, I also had to keep my eye on new bands for the label if I wanted to keep growing our roster. Managing talent on a record label is much like managing a baseball team. Baseball teams have positions to fill; you need good pitching and powerful hitting. You need to ensure every base is covered. Players get injured or fulfill their contracts and head elsewhere for more money or opportunity. Each season baseball managers have to find players who are free agents to fill the holes in their teams, whether it's a closing pitcher, a leadoff hitter, or a center fielder who can fire a baseball to the plate when someone is racing home. If the caliber of player that you want isn't available, you have to make do with what's out there. Labels are similar in that they need a well-rounded team to succeed.

With Bridge Nine, I could only grab the bands that hadn't been locked into an agreement with another label. I was only starting to warm up to this concept, since most of my releases until this point had been handshake deals. As the stakes and amount of money invested climbed for each project, it became necessary to protect the interests of both the artists and Bridge Nine, so contracts and lawyers became part of the process. I also needed a diverse style of bands from different places beyond Boston—Los Angeles, New York City, Europe. Working with artists in other cities created regional ambassadors and helped promote our efforts in their areas. I also wanted bands that were outspokenly straight edge, a lifestyle I still lived every day, and I needed a heavy band like Terror that knew how to work a crowd into a frenzy and ensure a constant flow of stage dives during every song.

I hoped Death Before Dishonor would fill the void that Terror left behind. They were cut from a similar cloth and were from close to home. If they became Boston's next significant export, I wanted to ensure they were waving the Bridge Nine flag. Their first record, *True till Death*, had come out the previous year, and while they were getting attention, I wasn't the biggest fan of how they were captured on recording and hadn't heard of anything else coming out of the studio where it was tracked. I'd seen them live, though, so I knew something was there.

They needed to get into a better studio with someone who could help tighten up their songs, and Jim Siegel at the Outpost was just the guy to do it. Under their new name, Give Up the Ghost, American Nightmare had recently recorded their second LP, *We're Down till We're Underground*, with Jim, and he'd produced albums with Death Threat, the Dropkick Murphys, and Blood for Blood—essentially a bunch of bands the guys in Death Before Dishonor had spent years listening to. Weeks earlier, I took a thousand dollars from Fenway sales to the post office and sent a money order to Jim as the deposit on their recording session. Shortly after, their Bridge Nine debut *Friends Family Forever* was delivered personally by Bryan, the band's vocalist. We sat at my desk at the Salem office and listened to the entire album. Every song was a banger. It still stung losing Terror, but Death Before Dishonor's heavy sound was an exciting step in the right direction that soothed the burn.

CHAPTER 23

I'm Just Messing with You

ONE EVENING, I WAS IN THE BOYLSTON STREET BUILDING GETting ready for that night's game when I got a call from Tiger.

"Hey, Chris," he said. "The Sox canceled our contract, so we won't be out tonight. I thought you should know."

I paused for a moment. Hearing that surprised me: I was initially happy we wouldn't have to worry about the Codees, but whatever was happening with their contract was surely temporary. What was going on?

Over the past few months, the Codees and our crew had come to an understanding. Pulling that "Killin' with Schillin'" tee at the mayor's request paid dividends. And by staying out of the range of Fenway Park's security staff and closed-circuit cameras, calls to the Codees had slowed down. We stood in our spots and sold shirts; they sat in a fast-food restaurant and didn't have to worry about us pissing off the souvenir stores. Everyone earned their paycheck with minimal fuss. That compromise made everyone's life easier, but to anyone working security at the stadium, it might've looked like we were no longer an issue.

Ah. *Now* it clicked why Tiger was giving me the heads-up: money.

"Got it," I replied. He didn't need to say it, but some cages needed rattling so the Red Sox would realize the Codees were worth the expense. This was a "devil you know" situation. I had earned a working relationship with the Codees, and without them around, the calls about us would be going to the Boston Police, who weren't going to give two shits about the politics of T-shirt vending. That scenario wouldn't be good for anyone.

The reality was that without the Codees keeping us in check, vendors would be posted up on the sidewalk at every exit leaving Fenway Park—just as we were about to be for that night's game. We'd give everyone a taste of the early days, hawking shirts from every corner of the park—T-shirts stretched across the hoods of cars parked alongside the stadium and hung from chain-link fences across the street, just below the windows of the Red Sox front offices.

We swarmed the exits and took back four years of lost ground in moments, slinging T-shirts over the shoulders of smiling customers and packing our pockets with cash. It was a triumphant return, if only for a single night as we sent a message for what every game would be like if the Codees weren't there to maintain the balance. The following day, I received a call from Tiger.

"Hey, Chris, it looks like the Red Sox need us after all; they reinstated us this morning. I'll see you tonight."

I chuckled as I hung up the phone. Our guerrilla selling tactics had worked; the balance was restored.

By this point, Bridge Nine's discography was well over fifty titles deep and showed no signs of slowing down. Cash flow was still tight as I waited for Lumberjack to pay us for months of reserves they owed, money that they held on to in case our releases were returned by stores within a specific time frame. I still managed to line up ten releases for 2004; I just had to lean harder into sports fans to earn the capital to make it all happen. In addition, Bridge Nine spent more than $20,000 to make fifty thousand copies of our

Hardcore 2004 sampler CD and had begun giving them away everywhere, ensuring everyone knew about our latest crop of bands.

Months earlier, half of the bands had played the annual Posi Numbers Fest in Wilkes-Barre, Pennsylvania, and footage from their performances was making the rounds. Hardcore-punk fans from all over the country had converged on a small club in rural Pennsylvania for three days, singing along with and stage diving to some of the best new bands in the genre. Talk about building a field of dreams; what did Wilkes-Barre have in common with the best hardcore bands in the world? It was all because one hardcore fan wanted to bring his favorite bands to his city. The early shows were in tiny VFW halls; years later, as attention grew, he began hosting the festival in larger and larger venues, drawing thousands of people. The weekend became so big that the city *itself* began to acknowledge and promote it.

The festival's palpable energy was captured by multiple camera angles. The videos posted online showed half of the crowd making it onto the stage and diving off. There were no barriers between the band and the audience. It was simultaneously chaotic and beautiful, everything I loved about hardcore punk. Many of our current heavy hitters were on the bill, and I'd go on to sign several more of the bands that played that weekend. Because of how busy my day-to-day workload was between both brands, I wasn't hitting the road as much anymore, and music festivals like this were becoming an opportunity to connect with a lot of people in a single weekend.

Elisabeth and I flew to Seattle the following week to help Champion celebrate releasing their first proper album, the *Promises Kept* LP. The Red Sox had a home stand with the visiting Texas Rangers that weekend that I would miss, but Max had Fenway covered and would keep things running for the few days I would be on the road. Everything was taken care of, so I could enjoy myself on the West Coast.

While we were out getting dinner with the band, my phone vibrated in my pocket. When I flipped it open, Tiger's name appeared across my screen.

He was three hours ahead of me on the East Coast, putting him right in the middle of a code-enforcement shift during the game at Fenway.

"Chris! Where are you?" he asked, his tone serious. "Aaron's been arrested. He's in the back of a squad car. He hit an undercover cop!"

"Wait, what?" None of what Tiger had said made sense. Aaron, the seller he was referencing, was one of the most mellow in our crew. He could talk shit with the best of them, but he wasn't throwing punches at anyone.

"They took him down to the ground and cuffed him!" Tiger continued. "This is wicked bad."

Jesus Christ, I thought, *of course shit starts when I'm on the other side of the country*. I was on the West Coast end of I-90, the same highway that became the Mass Pike once it hit Massachusetts. It started near Fenway Park and ended a few miles from where Champion's record-release show was about to go down.

"Did they take him to D-4?" I asked, referring to the police department that covered the Fenway neighborhood, where Matt had been transported in handcuffs on his first day as a vendor a couple of years earlier. My heart raced about dealing with this headache more than three thousand miles away, and I hoped Max had enough cash handy to bail him out. I didn't hear a response, so I asked, "Hey, Tiger, you there?"

After leaving me hanging for a moment, Tiger laughed loudly and said, "I'm just messing with you. Aaron's fine. See you when you get back!" He quickly hung up before I had a chance to respond.

I stared at my now silent phone. Goddammit, Tiger. You got me. He was fucking with me, but that had to be a good thing. My heart rate returned to normal.

CHAPTER 24

Believe in Boston

ELISABETH AND I LANDED IN BOSTON LATE SUNDAY NIGHT AS the Red Sox left for a seven-game road trip on the West Coast. They had been on a tear, winning eleven of their previous twelve games, but now that they were out of town it left me with no action at Fenway for the next week. Thankfully, there was a concert the following weekend at Fenway Park that was expected to draw almost as many fans as a Sox game, upwards of thirty-five thousand people.

A year earlier, the new ownership was eyeing every opportunity to make money, so they had begun experimenting with hosting other events in the stadium when the team was on the road. Bruce Springsteen had been the first to perform a concert the previous year, playing two sold-out shows in September 2003 and turning Fenway into "Bosston"—a golden T-shirt opportunity highlighting his nickname of "the Boss" if ever there was one. It was a gift I didn't grab, and I still regret missing that chance. Now, the second such concert was planned, this time with the mayor of Margaritaville, Jimmy Buffett, and I wasn't going to drop the ball if there was money to be made when his "License to Chill" tour made a two-show stop at Fenway Park.

I'd gotten pretty cocky over the previous couple of years selling so many T-shirts in the streets of Boston. I thought I could sell anything to anyone. Drunk Jimmy Buffett fans? Easy. Buffett and Boston had roughly the same number of letters and started with *B*. This wasn't rocket science, so I gave myself about twenty minutes to design something. First, I arched "BUFFETT" in a font similar to the one used by the Red Sox, added the dates of the concerts, and dropped in some cartoonish clip art of a parrot, a nod to his fans who were affectionately known as "Parrot Heads." The day before the first show, they were printed with red ink on a white shirt quickly and easily.

I pulled together a couple of guys to sell to the crowds headed into the concert and to the revelers who couldn't get in but could still enjoy the festive atmosphere on the sidewalk, as the music would no doubt reverberate throughout the neighborhood. One of the only complaints about the Bruce Springsteen concert the previous year had been the noise—you could hear his music as far away as Boston's South End. I wasn't expecting the Codees to be on duty, so we would run wild and hopefully get a few bonus sales days while the Sox were out of town. As we walked up to the bridge, Jimmy Buffett fans in their trademark Hawaiian shirts, straw hats, and colorful flower leis walked by. Lines of fans stretched from the entrances of bars, while others hung out on corners around the stadium, taking pictures in front of the Fenway Park facade.

The temperature was in the midseventies, and there wasn't a cloud in the sky as we pushed the little black T-shirt cart up against the rail of the bridge over the Mass Pike and started to assemble the display, stretching one of the T-shirts over the cardboard tube that acted as the shoulders and arms of a body form. I couldn't even get the cart fully up and running before I realized we were about to get blown out of the water by professional concert-shirt bootleggers. A crew from New York City had followed the band, and the T-shirts they were selling out of big black bags that hung from their shoulders put mine to such shame, it was comical. Their T-shirts were tie-dyed vibrantly with a rainbow of ink screen printed on both sides. A custom and exceptionally professional illustration of Fenway Park surrounded by parrots and flowers and the official tour branding made their shirts as nice as anything that was offered inside the stadium, and they were selling them for less than the fifteen dollars I'd hoped to get for my dinky little cut-and-paste joke of a concert tee. I was outgunned and would not make any money that night, but I couldn't even be mad. A complete strikeout, my boxes of Jimmy Buffett T-shirts were destined for donation to the Salvation Army on Route 1 in Saugus as a tax write-off at the end of the year. But didn't hockey great Wayne Gretzky famously say, "You miss 100 percent of the shots you don't take"? I was taking every shot I could. With Fenway Park being filled with people while the Red Sox were on the road, I needed to try to sell them something. I just needed to try harder next time.

The Buffett experiment proved I was better off sticking to what I knew, and, for the most part, that was contentious sports slogans: "Yankees Suck," "Yankee Hater," "A-Rod Is an A-Hole," "Steinbrenner Ruined Baseball," and "Take Your 26 Rings and Shove 'Em Up Your Ass," to name a few. In-your-face phrases had become my bread and butter, and with New York just three games ahead of Boston, there was a lot of Yanks-Sox talk, so the rivalry-fueling gear counted among my best-sellers. Unfortunately, the past two seasons had become a race to the bottom, with offerings from Sully's and the Suckers seemingly trying to outdo each other by getting even more aggressive and tasteless.

A few days before the Yankees returned to Fenway, the *Boston Globe* printed a story on the cover of the "Living Arts" section titled "Fenway Fandom Isn't Always Family-Friendly," which continued to a secondary headline of "Sox-Yankees Rivalry Earns an R Rating," while referencing some of the worst offenders being peddled to the crowds leaving the games. The article ensured that the Codees would catch heat from the Red Sox and have to crack some heads to show that they were doing their jobs. I felt a bit apprehensive about the next selling day, but I knew Tiger had my back.

On Friday, September 24, the Yankees arrived at Fenway for their regular-season showdown. I had walked the long way around the park, up over the bridge just north of the one that led into Kenmore Square. The 18-wheelers roared as they traveled past along the Mass Turnpike. Summer was still holding on, and the breeze was warm as the sun began to set. As I neared the corner where we usually set up, I noticed a commotion in the parking lot behind the apartment buildings overlooking Kenmore Square.

It was 7:55 p.m., and the Suckers had parked their van in a loading zone; the back doors were open, boxes of shirts had been stacked on the pavement between carts, and a few vendors had been unloading them to prepare for the postgame crowd. Standing to the other side of the van were two Codees, enforcing the "8:00 p.m." rule. The Suckers knew it was a bullshit bust; it was only a few minutes until 8:00, and they weren't even out on the sidewalk; this was all happening in a private parking lot behind an apartment building. Their outrage was disregarded, as the Codees impounded a good chunk of their inventory for the weekend. It was an expensive strike against them, seeing as the Yankees would be in town for three games, forcing the Suckers to return to their storage unit and scrounge whatever they could sell if they would make any money. I shook my head, thankful it wasn't me, and kept walking until I reached the corner parking lot next to the Bank of America. A curb between the lot and the sidewalk awaited me to sit on it until people started leaving the stadium.

Pedro Martínez was on the mound and gave up five runs to the Yankees through the eighth inning, which was eerily familiar to what had happened to him during the 2003 ALCS after being kept in too long. Fans began to head out during the top of the ninth inning as the Yankees added a few more runs to take the lead, but customers eagerly lined up, and I still killed it that night, in significant part due to the Suckers not being around. During the postgame interview, Pedro addressed his poor performance and, in an attempt to make light of it, said, "What can I say, just tip my hat and call the Yankees my Daddy." Goddamn, Pedro, I thought. You're just giving away money to the people like us making shirts in the Bronx with a quote like that.

The next night, I went from a street vendor dodging the Codees to a businessman presenting a charity check on-field with the WFNX radio crew. After the Sox-Yankees bench-clearing brawl months earlier, right fielder Gabe Kapler was penalized $2,500 for tangling with Yankees pitcher Tanyon Sturtze, who had emerged from the fight with a bloody cheek. My friend Chris Rucker, a longtime hardcore-punk fan who curated a local music show on WFNX and had been instrumental in bringing Slapshot to the label, reached out to me to have Sully's create a T-shirt for the station to sell to raise money to help "pay" Gabe's fine. Collectively, we presented the donation with a five-foot ceremonial check at home plate before the game. It was a chance to do something good that legitimized the brand. It felt great as I stared out at the crowds from the perspective usually reserved for the players; for the first time, I was on the inside looking out. I enjoyed every second of it. I may have only been a hundred yards from the sidewalk where I'd spent the past five years grinding it out after every game, hustling merch to baseball fans, but it felt like I was a thousand miles away.

As I walked off the field, my cell phone began to buzz. It was Tiger.

"Chris, was that you on the field just now?"

"Hey, Tiger!" I responded. "Yeah, we raised money for Kapler's charity."

"I thought so," he laughed. "I told someone from the Red Sox that I thought it was you down there with the check, and they didn't look happy."

"Well, they should get used to it," I replied, because I knew I was only getting started. Sully's was no longer a means to an end for Bridge Nine.

It was supporting the label financially, but as a separate company, it had so much potential. At first, the only place to grab a Sully's shirt was on the street, but it was becoming a brand with name recognition translating into serious sales.

I began doubling down on advertising, dropping 2,500 bucks on a full-page ad in the popular free alternative weekly *Boston Phoenix* newspaper. I spent another $2,400 on radio commercials with WFNX to let fans know that *our* shirts were ones they needed to grab when they headed home after a game. Our online store gained traction, and orders were coming in from all over the country. Retailers began stocking Sully's T-shirts, first in the souvenir store owned by our landlord and then in Newbury Comics stores all over New England, after I began soliciting the brand to the buyers who were taking in Bridge Nine's releases. Revenue from our website and from wholesale accounts soon outpaced what I earned on the street.

As I made changes to beef up the Bridge Nine roster, the Red Sox adjusted theirs to be as competitive as possible in the second half of their season. At the July 31 MLB trade deadline, statistics-driven Red Sox general manager Theo Epstein made a trade that had previously been unthinkable, sending away shortstop Nomar Garciaparra—a popular but injury-prone player more commonly known in Boston as "Nomahhh" who had been a face of the franchise—in a deal that helped augment the team's defense and better prepare them for the final stretch. The trade worked. During August, the Sox won twenty-one games and lost only seven, a dramatic improvement from the .500 ball they had been playing from May through July. Holes in the 2003 team were being filled so as not to let history repeat itself *if* the Red Sox made it to the postseason for the second consecutive year.

September had seen the Red Sox hold their own, and the hits kept coming, with eighteen wins and just ten losses. They split their last six games with the Yankees, with each team winning three apiece, but New York was three games ahead in the standings and went on to win the American League

East Division title for the seventh year in a row. The Red Sox did, however, qualify for the wild-card spot again as they had in 2003, a second chance to get into the World Series by taking on the Western Division–winning Anaheim Angels. I started the best-of-five series by ordering a thousand T-shirts. The series saw the Red Sox take the first three games and win the ALDS, while the Yankees battled the Minnesota Twins, the Central Division champions. Despite the Yankees losing Game One, they returned and took the next three, setting the stage for a rematch of the Yankees and Red Sox in the ALCS and another chance for Boston to finally win it all.

The Red Sox and the Yankees would face off for a best-of-seven series that October—and we were ready for it. A majority of Boston's most active hardcore-punk musicians were represented among our crew: Kevin from the Hope Conspiracy, Luke from Fastbreak, Azy from Panic, Greg and Dan from Mental, Ten Yard Fight and In My Eyes founding member Tony Pops who was now in Sinners & Saints, Nick and Chris from Some Kind of Hate, Tommy from Cops and Robbers. So many bands had a connection to the hustle.

Major League Baseball's suits must have seen the volume of T-shirts being sold in Boston that riffed on the rivalry with New York because they let a licensee run with Pedro Martínez's "Daddy" quote, shipping officially licensed T-shirts that had "Hey Red Sox, Who's Your Daddy?" printed over the image of a baby's pacifier with a Yankees logo on it to stores all over New York. MLB's senior vice president of merchandising, Howard Smith, said, "Fans want an *attitudinal product*." Well, no kidding! It took only five full seasons and us collectively selling north of a hundred thousand T-shirts disparaging the Yankees for MLB to realize that fans wanted to talk smack on their rivals even more than they wanted to rep their home team.

Unlike Sully's, which catered only to Boston fans and didn't care what New York fans thought, the blowback was immediate. The shirt was pulled from shelves shortly after its release when enough people complained.

After sweeping the Angels, the Red Sox had good momentum, and fans were nervously optimistic. Still, during the Divisional Series, the Red Sox suffered a setback that had the potential to affect their postseason ambitions. Pitching ace Curt Schilling suffered a torn tendon after being hit by a line drive in Game One. He returned one week later at Yankee Stadium in Game One of the ALCS, and the results were disastrous, giving up six runs in the first three innings with the Red Sox losing 7–10. Game Two had the Yankees holding the lead for the entire game, winning 3–1. Game Three had the series return to Fenway Park, but the Yankees took that game in a dramatic 19–8 routing over the Red Sox in an eerily similar score to the "1918" chant Yankees fans kept bellowing as the runs stacked up for New York. It was the most lopsided postseason loss in Sox history.

I had ordered sixteen hundred T-shirts to prepare for the series and already regretted it. I also pulled the trigger on a $1,700 plane ticket to Australia so I could accompany Champion on their first tour Down Under. If the Red Sox got eliminated, paying the credit-card bill for that the following month was going to hurt. It appeared the season was over, and we dropped the price of our T-shirts as Red Sox fans poured out of Fenway Park during the early innings to move whatever we could.

No baseball team had ever come back to win a best-of-seven series after losing the first three games, and no one was counting on the Red Sox to be the first. Game Four took place in the evening of October 17—Edge Day. Longtime *Boston Globe* columnist Dan Shaughnessy wrote, "For the 86th consecutive autumn, the Red Sox are not going to win the World Series" on the front page of that day's newspaper. It was over. I felt it was time to start focusing on T-shirts for hockey fans because the Bruins had started their season on the road the night before and were returning to the Garden in just four days.

That night, one of the vendors had brought a small AM/FM radio and hung it from the branch of a small tree in front of the Bank of America. All

Kenmore Square vendors huddled around it, hanging on every word as the announcer detailed each play. We could hear the cheers and boos coming from inside the stadium first, and a moment later, the delayed radio broadcast gave context to what was happening.

The Yankees scored twice in the third inning, and Red Sox fans were already leaving the stadium. They couldn't stomach watching their team lose it all once again. In the fifth inning, the Red Sox bounced back and scored three times to take the lead, but the excitement was fleeting, as they gave up two more runs in the sixth, with the Yankees keeping the lead through the first half of the ninth inning.

We continued attempting to sell T-shirts at a deep discount. Getting even five dollars for a shirt was better than having it sit in a bin collecting dust for the next six months. It was a desperate attempt; most Sox fans were no longer emotionally equipped to care about anything related to baseball. The odds said the Red Sox were done, heading into the bottom of the ninth inning a run behind the Yankees, with future first-ballot Baseball Hall of Famer Mariano Rivera back on the mound. Rivera allowed a rare leadoff walk with no outs on the board, putting Kevin Millar on first. Dave Roberts, a midseason trade with a near-perfect record of stealing second base, replaced Kevin as a pinch runner. After multiple attempts by Rivera to pick him off at first, Roberts successfully stole second, putting himself in scoring position. Every fan inside Fenway Park jumped out of their seats when Red Sox third baseman Bill Mueller blasted the next pitch, knocking Rivera on his ass while it rolled into center field, allowing Roberts to score and tie the game, narrowly staving off elimination.

The following two and a half innings were a draw; the score remained tied until the bottom of the twelfth inning when Manny Ramirez crushed a ball into left field, getting on base. It was after one in the morning, and we were all exhausted. We'd been standing on the sidewalk with our shirt carts all night, and the last wave of fans leaving had been hours earlier. Now everyone was glued to the game to see what would happen next as we listened to each pitch on the radio moments after it happened.

Then, all of a sudden, a thunderous roar of cheers came from the stadium, and we could hear the first few notes of "Dirty Water" begin to play, signaling a Red Sox win. We all ran back to our carts, jumping and shouting, "Yes! Yes!" as the sound of car horns honking to acknowledge the win echoed around us. We prepared to sell as many shirts as possible to the remaining fans, who, by sticking it out in the stadium, had just seen an incredible two-run blast by David "Big Papi" Ortiz into the Yankees bullpen in right field, extending the series by at least another game. Shirts we were practically giving away two innings earlier were now going for twenty dollars, and the vendors with "Big Papi" T-shirts in their carts did the most business after his late-night (or early-morning, as it were) heroics. At Max Powers's urging, I had been the first to put Ortiz's nickname on a T-shirt over an illustration of his hands making his trademark point to the heavens after a home run like the one he'd had tonight.

Game Five saw the Red Sox score twice in the first inning, but their bats remained silent for most of the game, as the Yankees put four runs on the board. They tied it in the bottom of the eighth inning and then got deadlocked as the game went another five and a half innings without a run by either team. David Ortiz attained hero status once again after he got a base hit and brought home outfielder Johnny Damon, giving the Sox the win in the bottom of the fourteenth inning. Damon had grown his hair down to his shoulders and wore a beard, prompting many to say he looked like Jesus Christ. "Jesus Is My Homeboy" was a trendy T-shirt, so I made a parody version featuring Johnny Damon that said "Damon Is My Homeboy" and sold thousands of them until a fan wearing one was featured on the broadcast of a Yankees and Red Sox game. This unexpected and highly viewed exposure led to a flurry of cease-and-desist letters from Damon's agent, the MLB Players Association, and the company that made the T-shirt that had inspired it, forcing it into retirement. It was a short-lived design, but its proceeds paid to record most of Champion's *Promises Kept* and Death Before Dishonor's *Friends Family Forever* albums, and both bands fueled much of the interest in Bridge Nine going into the new year.

The Red Sox took two of the three games at Fenway Park and were headed back to the Bronx for Game Six, where they had won roughly only one of every three games played there in 2004. Fans were anxiously excited, but the statistic that no baseball team had ever come back from a 0–3 deficit weighed heavily. Curt Schilling was back on the mound and had experience dealing with the Yankees in the postseason. He had previously defeated them in the 2001 World Series with the Arizona Diamondbacks, earning an MVP Award.

Curt's injured tendon was still a liability, so the Red Sox team physician developed a radical procedure to help allow him to pitch. It involved using three stitches to secure his tendon to the skin of his ankle, keeping the tendon in place so that it wouldn't painfully shift over the bone as he pitched. The operation was first tried on a cadaver and then on Curt the day before he was set to start in New York. When he walked out to the mound during Game Six, the television cameras zoomed in on his feet, showing what appeared to be blood soaking through the now symbolically red sock on the ankle of his right foot. Red Sox Nation held their collective breath, wore their hats inside out, knocked on wood, and pandered to any superstition they believed could help summon a much-needed win for Boston.

The game might have been in New York, but back in Boston, the crowds in the neighborhood around Fenway Park considerably increased as fans looked for places to assemble to watch the game and be a part of the historical record written on the field in the Bronx. Lines of forty people or more stretched in front of bars until they reached their capacity; any with a TV screen within view of the front windows attracted large groups of people hoping to catch each play and keep track of the score. When the Sox got a hit, arms shot up in celebration and fans jumped in the air; when they struck out to end an inning and left players on base, you'd hear a round of "Fuck!" and "Goddamn it!" as people looked down and clutched their heads in frustration. We were there all the while to keep the T-shirts flowing.

The procedure for Curt Schilling's tendon was a success, and despite the red sock, he pitched as if he was at 100 percent. The Red Sox scored four runs in the fourth inning and kept the Yankees off the board until the seventh, when Schilling gave up a home run and was replaced by Bronson Arroyo. In the bottom of the eighth inning, A-Rod hit a ground ball to Arroyo, who scooped it up and ran up the first-base line to tag Rodriguez out. A-Rod slapped the ball out of Bronson's hand, and Derek Jeter scored before the play was reviewed and ultimately overturned by the umpires who convened on the field. Jeter returned to first base, A-Rod was called out, and one of our future best-selling T-shirts wrote itself: "A-Rod Slaps Balls."

The Yankees scored again, but the Red Sox won 4–2. It was euphoric and unbelievable. Game Six had seen the Red Sox hold the lead for the full nine innings, unlike the first three games, where stressed-out Boston fans found themselves on the edge of their seats. For many people, it was the first time in a week they could breathe. No one, and I mean no one, thought the Red Sox could win three straight to force a Game Seven after they dropped the first three, and if they said otherwise, they were lying.

WEDNESDAY, OCTOBER 20, 2004. Game Seven was must-see TV. The Yankees and Red Sox face-off was the only thing anyone could talk about. The whole city was electric, and the fan bandwagon was in full effect; people who'd never been to a game before were suddenly talking about the World Series. Like the previous night, long lines stretched from every bar and restaurant that would be broadcasting the game. It looked as though the game was happening in Boston, as fans from all over made the pilgrimage to the Fenway neighborhood to be close to the home of the Red Sox, despite the action happening two hundred miles away at Yankee Stadium.

To remind the Red Sox of one of the more bitter moments in their shared history, the Yankees invited retired player Bucky Dent—who'd won the World Series MVP Award shortly after his three-run homer helped end Boston's 1978 season—to throw the ceremonial first pitch before the game. If they were trying to shake the Red Sox, they would have to do better than that because, in the top of the first inning, a David Ortiz home run into the right-field bleachers brought him and Manny Ramirez home for a 2–0 lead. The second inning saw Johnny Damon grand slam the first pitch he saw into right field, and within one and a half innings, the score was Red Sox 6, Yankees 0. This early in the game, and Sox fans were enjoying an uncharacteristic break from the usual pressure? They were *not* used to that.

The Yankees got one run in the bottom of the third, but Boston responded again, with Johnny Damon getting his second home run of the game, bringing in shortstop Orlando Cabrera and making the score 8–1. The extra runs were insurance that helped Boston fans relax, but they were still playing the same team that had scored nineteen times just days earlier, so nothing could be taken for granted. In words attributed to catching legend Yogi Berra, who spent twenty-nine seasons with the Yankees as a player, coach, and manager between 1946 and 1983, "It ain't over till it's over."

In the bottom of the seventh, Pedro Martínez was on the mound to continue what starting pitcher Derek Lowe had accomplished so far, allowing only one run and one hit. Chants of "Who's your daddy?" echoed throughout Yankee Stadium. He ultimately allowed two runs in, but it could have been worse. The Yankees inched up the scoreboard but still trailed by five runs.

Second baseman Mark Bellhorn started the eighth inning with a solo home run, adding to the Red Sox lead, while the next three batters were retired in order. The Yankees' top three hitters were dealt with equally decisively; Derek Jeter grounded out to the third base, A-Rod struck out, and Gary Sheffield grounded out to the shortstop. The Red Sox were one inning away from heading to the World Series, but that didn't slow the racing hearts of Boston fans nationwide who were glued to the broadcast, afraid their team would find a way to fuck it up again. The ghosts of postseasons past haunted every Red Sox fan watching. Bucky *fucking* Dent and his home run in the tiebreaker with the Yankees in 1978. The ground ball that went through Bill Buckner's legs in the 1986 World Series with the Mets. Aaron Boone's devastating home run in the bottom of the eleventh inning one year earlier during Game Seven of the 2003 ALCS that sent the Yankees to another World Series appearance—where at least they ended up losing to the Florida Marlins. Boston would repeatedly get so close and then have it ripped away.

In the top of the ninth, the Red Sox got one more run from a sacrifice–fly ball before the first half of the inning ended. They'd managed to put ten runs on the board. Was that enough? They had stepped up in all the right spots throughout the second half of the series, and now they were down to one last half of an inning.

Yankee outfielder Hideki Matsui hit the fourth pitch by Red Sox relief pitcher Mike Timlin into right field, putting him on first. Center fielder Bernie Williams waited until he had a full count to hit a ground ball right to Mark Bellhorn, who threw it to Orlando Cabrera at second to force Matsui out. One down, two to go. Up next was catcher Jorge Posada, the subject of our wildly popular "Posada Is A Little Bitch" T-shirt, which we had debuted five months earlier. I'd sold thousands over the season. Posada wasn't a little guy—he stood six feet, two inches tall—but it was just another way to talk smack with a T-shirt, and Red Sox fans tripped over themselves to buy them.

Posada popped it up, and Cabrera caught the second out. They needed just one more. Yankee Stadium was filled with pensive-looking New Yorkers, while the Red Sox fans in the Fenway neighborhood excitedly lost their minds seeing the Yankees on the ropes. Spurred on by the decisive lead that the Red Sox had early in the game, students from the colleges around the Fenway neighborhood started arriving in greater and greater numbers to be a part of the festive atmosphere. Over each of their heads, we just saw floating dollar signs.

After Yankees designated hitter Kenny Lofton was walked, and there were now two men on base, Timlin was pulled and relief pitcher Alan Embree entered to finish the job. Yankee pinch hitter Rubén Sierra hit the second pitch he saw, sending it right at Mark Bellhorn, who threw it to Kevin Millar at first to get the last out.

Holy shit—the Yankees lost! The Yankees *fucking lost*!

Every Red Sox fan waited their entire lives for the chance to watch the Yankees get knocked on their ass, and it had finally happened. Fans howled in celebration and thanked their gods.

The Red Sox had done it! Against all odds, they became the first Major League Baseball team to overcome a three-game-to-zero deficit in a best-of-seven postseason series. Twenty-five other teams going back to 1907 had tried and failed before them, and the Red Sox were the only ones to come back and win it all. The Yankees had four chances to finish the Red Sox and had blown each one, night after night. The 2004 ALCS had seen Boston finally defeat their rivals in the postseason, as the Yankees choked in the biggest upset that baseball had ever seen.

As tens of thousands of fans at Yankee Stadium looked on, the rest of the Red Sox ran onto the field, hugging each other and celebrating. Sox fans rushed into the streets in Boston, clogging them with an estimated eighty thousand people. The "Yankees suck!" chant filled the air around Fenway Park and grew louder with every refrain. And finally, it wasn't being said out of bitterness. It was true. The Yankees *sucked*. The Yankees *fucking sucked*. For the first time since 1986, the Boston Red Sox would return to the World Series and were one step closer to busting the Curse. It was glorious.

Exhilaration swept through Red Sox Nation, and everywhere that fans gathered, they partied and rejoiced, vanquishing what had haunted them for generations. Strangers hugged and high-fived each other. People cried for joy, and others danced on the sidewalk. Backyard fireworks left over from the Fourth of July shot up throughout the city, colorfully exploding in the midnight sky as honking car horns could be heard in every direction.

CHAPTER 25

Redemption

THE RED SOX HAD DEFEATED THE YANKEES, BUT IT WOULD BE a hollow victory unless they went on to win the 2004 World Series, where they faced the St. Louis Cardinals. Boston's postseason history with St. Louis had been as heartbreaking as with New York. The teams rarely met, but when they had—in 1946 and 1967—the Red Sox made it all the way to Game Seven before losing. Fans hoped the outcome with the Cardinals would be different from what their parents and grandparents had experienced.

Game One was held on October 23 at Fenway Park. The game began on a solemn note, as the celebration in the streets around Fenway Park a few nights earlier had taken an unfortunate and tragic turn. Some people hid in the anonymity of the crowd and began to knock over garbage cans, setting small fires in the streets, and jumping on top of cars. Mob mentality around those early instigators set in, and people once again attempted to flip cars over; at least one with New York plates became fully engulfed in flames just blocks from our office. If it was climbable, fans hung from it, whether it was a street sign or the facade of a building. An army of police officers wearing head-to-toe riot gear responded, many with "less-than-lethal" guns that shot pepper bullets to break up the crowds. Emerson College student Victoria Snelgrove was mortally wounded when she was shot in the eye with one of these bullets and later succumbed to her injuries. A moment of silence in Victoria Snelgrove's memory was observed before the game, along with a plea to stop the violence. The Dropkick Murphys returned to perform "Tessie," with hopes of keeping the positive vibes from the historic ALCS going. The city no longer allowed bars to keep long lines outside, and once their capacity was met, anyone left waiting was asked to keep moving, not allowed to congregate on the streets. After a crowd of about fifteen people cheered while watching the game through the large windows of the Boston Beer Works bar, police spoke with the staff, who then hung a large white tarp to block the view of the TVs inside.

Boston put four runs on the board in the bottom of the first inning, and Fenway Park was rocking and rolling. The Cardinals responded with a run apiece in the top of the second and third innings, but the Red Sox returned with three more in the bottom of the third. St. Louis managed to tie it up at 7–7 in the sixth inning, but Boston pulled ahead and took Game One, 11–9.

Before Game Two, the three surviving members of the 1946 Red Sox team that had faced the Cardinals in that year's series collectively threw out the first pitch. Curt Schilling was on the mound with his stitched-up ankle for the first six innings and allowed no earned runs; the only Cardinal who scored did so after an error by the Red Sox. Boston won 6–2. They were up 2–0 in the best-of-seven series, and fans were elated. So were we. Despite the overbearing presence of body armor–clad police near Fenway Park, we made record sales.

In Game Three, Boston headed to St. Louis. There they scored four times in the first five innings, kicking things off with a home run by Manny Ramirez. St. Louis managed to snag only a single run in the bottom of the ninth before the Red Sox won. Despite being up 3–0 in the series, anything could still happen.

Game Four had the Red Sox working to close out the series with a sweep in St. Louis. Johnny Damon hit a home run during the first Red Sox at-bat. Hits by David Ortiz and Trot Nixon drove in two more runs during the third inning. Both teams put zeros on the board for the next six innings. The Red Sox loaded the bases in the eighth, but the Cardinals got out of the inning without letting any more runs in.

In the bottom of the ninth inning, Red Sox closing pitcher Keith Foulke was on the mound. Cardinals slugger Albert Pujols started the inning by blasting a ground ball through Foulke's legs, conjuring up memories of Bill Buckner in the 1986 World Series with the Mets. Red Sox fans winced despite the commanding series lead. There were no outs yet, and the two batters were retired with a pop-up to right field and a strikeout, respectively. Two down. A single out remained between the Red Sox and their long-sought World Series win. The first pitch to Cardinals shortstop Édgar Rentería was inside and caused him to jump back a bit from the plate. Rentería had recorded hits in two of his three at-bats during the game, and he was St. Louis's best hope to extend the series to a Game Five. Pujols took second base and got into scoring position. Red Sox fans held their breath but didn't have to for long, as Rentería bounced the ball to Foulke on the second pitch he saw. The pitcher reached up and grabbed the baseball in his glove, ran part of the way to first base, and tossed it to Doug Mientkiewicz to record the final out of the game. Each member of the 2004 Red Sox team jumped into the air in celebration, followed by every one of their fans. Fox Sports commentator Joe Buck famously reported in the game's final moments: *"Red Sox fans have longed to hear it. The Boston Red Sox are world champions!"*

Boston had first overcome the greatest of odds against New York and then made winning the World Series look easy, sweeping St. Louis and celebrating in their stadium. And with that, it was official; the Red Sox had busted the eighty-six-year Curse. The team rushed the field for the second time in a week, now as World Series Champions. Each member became a hero in Boston. There would be no more talk about Babe Ruth and curses, and if a Yankees fan ever dared chant "1918" again, the proper response would be "2004."

Fenway's street vendors had to forfeit our chance to sell in Boston while the Sox found redemption in St. Louis, since a near battalion of riot police seven hundred strong had taken over the streets surrounding the stadium. They were not giving the tens of thousands of revelers an inch. They swept the streets shoulder to shoulder and pushed fans out of the area.

SATURDAY, OCTOBER 30, 2004. The festivities continued with a rolling rally-style parade weaving through the streets of Boston from Fenway Park and downtown, a relatively new tradition that had started after the New England Patriots won their first Super Bowl two years earlier. The city of Boston contracted Boston Duck Tours, a company that gave historical tours on World War II–era amphibious vehicles, to host the Patriots in 2002, and again this past spring after they beat the Carolina Panthers in Super Bowl XXXVIII. The "Duck Boats," as they were known, were perfect for the event, their wide decks allowing for players, coaches, and staff to stand and wave to the throngs of crowds as they slowly drove through the city. Despite the overcast and inclement weather, an estimated three million people were expected to come to see the parade. The Liberated crew worked around the clock printing more than eight thousand T-shirts, many of which were boxed up and loaded into a rental truck to bring to the tent we had secured on the sidewalk in front of our building at the start of the parade route. By six in the morning, we were stacking piles of "Believe in Boston" shirts on folding tables and preparing for a day of hawking to fans who still couldn't believe the Red Sox had won it all. Shortly after everything was up and running, Tiger and another Codee walked up to the tent. We were set up as an extension of the retail store owned by my landlord, who had been a fixture in the neighborhood since the 1970s, but we were still open to being fucked with should someone want to.

"Hey, Tiger!" I said as he strolled over. "Think the rain will hold out?"

"Yeah, you should be good for a bit," he replied, then added: "I'm getting reports that the guys from New York are here with counterfeits, so we're looking for them. Let me know if you see anything." He glanced around at our tables and, with a wink, said, "Good luck. I hope you sell it all!" He then continued walking up Boylston Street along the parade route. It looked like the locals were getting a much-needed pass today, while the bootleggers who had come from out of state to sell bogus World Series Champion Red Sox shirts along the parade route would be getting the Codees' full attention.

As the parade started, the crowd began to roar as the first police motorcycles approached, a line of Duck Boats stretching down the street behind them. Confetti was blown out of cannons, twirling and fluttering down on the spectators and poncho-wearing police officers walking alongside the Duck Boats. I was wearing the cash backpack and could feel the weight of the money we'd already raked in, and it was only ten in the morning. The crowds along the route alternated chants of "Let's go, Red Sox!" with "Yankees suck!" The parade would soon pass by our tent, but this last hoorah of selling T-shirts to Red Sox fans was only getting started. I loaded up backpacks and carts full of T-shirts and, one by one, sent them out with people who would work the crowds farther along the parade route, giving instructions not to return until they sold absolutely everything.

As the crowds of fans around our tent dispersed, I headed downstairs into the building. I swung the bag off my shoulder, placing it in front of me so I could unzip it. Turning it upside down over the sizable polished wood conference table in the center of the room, I shook it as thick wads of cash spilled out and spread across the table. I pulled out the largest bills first, straightening and stacking them before me. After sorting the hundreds and fifties, I moved to the twenty-dollar bills, counting and arranging them in stacks of a thousand—one after another, wrapping a rubber band around each folded bundle. I had tens of thousands of dollars laid out on the table. Seeing the return from our efforts spread out like that was an incredible rush. Each thousand-dollar bundle had started as four dozen T-shirts, but would become so much more. A few more days in a recording studio. Another magazine advertisement. A deposit on filming a music video or a commercial that would air on MTV. Tour support for a band headed to Europe for a month of shows so they could pay some bills at home. A dozen new bands would benefit from the Red Sox winning it all. And there was even enough left over to renovate the bathroom in the condo Elisabeth and I shared.

CHAPTER 26

Five Years Later

THE YEAR 2009 WAS SHAPING UP TO BE BRIDGE NINE'S BUSIEST, with nearly two dozen new releases. I was working with many of the most popular bands in the genre. I'd even negotiated a special twenty-fifth-year anniversary release with Agnostic Front, a band known as the "Godfathers of New York Hardcore," for their debut album, *Victim in Pain*. That was coming out in November, and the irony of reissuing one of the most important albums from New York City's first generation of hardcore punks, on a Boston-based label originally fueled by anti–New York Yankee sentiments, was not lost on me.

The label's staff had increased to seven, and we were operating out of a ten-thousand-square-foot warehouse in Peabody, having moved from Salem two years earlier in search of room to grow at a reasonable rent. Salem had been nice, but maybe *too* nice. Down the hall from us had been state offices, with our heavily tattooed staff seen as misfits. When the rent was about to increase for the second consecutive year, I moved us to a granite-wall, wood-beam pre–Civil War mill building with all the space we could need one town over and at half the cost per square foot.

The Peabody building, while lacking some of the creature comforts of our previous office, also housed Sully's and Liberated Images. Collectively, there were fifteen of us working alongside each other, a wild accomplishment because eight years earlier, it had been just me, and between the brands we were on pace to do more than $2 million in sales this year, a staggering number for someone who had started his record label in a dorm room. Elisabeth and I were still living in a two-bedroom condo and sharing her car, so it didn't feel like I was selling millions of dollars' worth of records and T-shirts. Any profit went back into the business, funding its growth, so I didn't have much to show for it at home outside of an updated bathroom. But anything seemed possible, and every new opportunity was bigger than the one before it.

Sully's had enjoyed a wave of good fortune, as Boston sports continued to come out on top for the past few years. The Red Sox returned to the World Series in 2007 and swept it again, winning all four games against the Colorado Rockies. The past spring the Boston Celtics won their first NBA finals in twenty-two years, taking the series against their rivals, the Los Angeles Lakers, in six games. Both championships and their subsequent celebratory parades meant big bucks for Sully's, and I flooded the city with "Believe in Boston" merchandise.

The 2009 Red Sox season ended earlier in the week when they were eliminated at Fenway Park by the Angels in the ALDS. They'd lost the first two games of the series but had pulled ahead and were leading 6–4 in Game Three, until they gave up three runs in the top of the ninth inning, ultimately being swept in the series. On the other hand, the Yankees had finally made it past their own ALDS for the first time since 2004 and were playing Game Two against the Los Angeles Dodgers at Yankee Stadium. Despite the loss of income at Fenway, the Bruins were already three weeks into their season, and the Celtics would be hitting the parquet floors at the Garden in a couple of weeks. The money was guaranteed to keep flowing.

Sully's continued to diversify and entered the publishing world, releasing the 352-page tome *One Fan's Story: If This Hat Could Talk* by our employee (and "Massachusetts governor of Red Sox Nation") Jared Carrabis. Jared was a blogging Red Sox superfan who had recognized the potential of social media for sports teams before the actual leagues did, building a MySpace page that had amassed more than one hundred thousand followers. That caught my attention, leading to a job offer to Jared and, ultimately, to his first publishing deal. To kick off the book's release, Jared participated in a meet-and-greet at his hometown Newbury Comics store in Saugus to sign and sell copies of his new book.

Liberated Images was firing on all cylinders, having finally invested in a fully automated screen-printing press the previous summer, thanks to the Boston Red Sox going all the way. The crew at Liberated had printed every shirt sold during the 2007 World Series by hand but finally acquired an eight-head $90,000 fully auto press and a twenty-five-foot gas oven for curing the shirts. Our print capacity more than tripled, and we were customizing apparel for bands all over Massachusetts and up and down the East Coast. All three businesses had come a long way from their bootstrapped beginnings and were being recognized for their rapid growth. The *Improper Bostonian* magazine crowned Bridge Nine the city's "Record Label of the Year" for 2009.

SATURDAY, OCTOBER 17, 2009. The parking lot outside of the Wonderland Ballroom in Revere was filled with cars and clean-cut hardcore-punk fans. Groups hung out around the trunks of their vehicles, waiting for the lines at the entrance of the building to move. That would take some time, as each line was several hundred people deep, and getting into the venue took longer than anyone had expected. Each person's name had to be checked off a will-call list before they were admitted inside, delaying entry.

Have Heart was performing later that night, headlining a stacked bill with all of their friends' bands, including Bane, Foundation, Shipwreck, and Cruel Hand, who were opening the show and had already begun playing to the handful of people who had made it in. It was Have Heart's highly promoted and anticipated final show, and it was being held on Edge Day, ten years to the day from Ten Yard Fight's final performance at the Karma Club in 1999. The date had been chosen so they could continue the tradition of bands playing one last time on the day now recognized internationally as acknowledging "straight edge."

The last few years were good for Have Heart, whose two full-length albums were released on Bridge Nine. The 2006 album *The Things We Carry* and 2008's *Songs to Scream at the Sun* were already modern-day hardcore-punk classics, and the band had toured the entire world supporting them. In fact, since May 2009, they'd performed their music in China and Southeast Asia, Australia, and North, Central, and South America, and they'd spent a month in Europe. They even booked five shows in Africa. I hadn't known any hardcore bands to make it to Africa yet. Even as they were calling it quits, they were still blazing new trails.

Have Heart had become the best-selling band on Bridge Nine, and they had become a part of a growing wave of artists getting a taste of commercial success while performing fast and heavy music. Over the past few years, albums on the label were starting to enter the mainstream, with new releases from Have Heart, Death Before Dishonor, H2O, and New Found Glory breaking into the *Billboard* album top sales charts. Death Before Dishonor's music video for the song "Break Through It All" was in regular rotation on MTV's *Headbanger's Ball*. And a nationwide US "Bridge Nine" label tour was winding its way through the Midwest to California, featuring recent signing Strike Anywhere with support from Crime in Stereo, Ruiner, and Polar Bear Club, all of whom had just released new music.

Hardcore-punk fans were filing in and filling the open dance floor inside the Wonderland Ballroom. The venue was better known for its reggae- and Latin-themed music nights, but the promoters of those events had been dealing with episodes of violence, culminating in five people being stabbed on a single February night in 2005. Most nightclubs where alcohol flows freely and bravado is unchecked will eventually deal with the occasional act of violence, but five people stabbed? Concerned citizens and city councillors turned the proverbial screws and lobbied for the city to pull the venue's liquor license, which many felt fueled the problem. Ultimately, the bar was forced to close an hour earlier than usual, leading to smaller crowds and profits.

With the sudden loss of business, it didn't take a rocket scientist to realize hardcore-punk shows would fill some of the void less than two months later. Throughout the rest of 2005, bands like Mental, Madball, Paint It Black, and Wes Eisold's new hardcore-punk outfit, Some Girls, headlined nights, ensuring decent-size crowds that didn't mind the earlier closing time. Often referred to as Club Lido, the name of the smaller capacity venue inside the entertainment complex, the Wonderland Ballroom had opened its stages to many of the world's biggest and best hardcore bands. And just the past month, it hosted what had been promoted as "The Great American Hardcore Fest," which featured forty-two bands, including Have Heart. Now the band was returning for one final performance to play to thousands of fans who'd traveled worldwide to send them off.

The opening bands had worked the room into a fervor, with mirrors on the walls and camera lenses of those documenting the evening fogged from the damp heat. T-shirts wet with sweat clung to the fans still wearing them as nearly two thousand people waited patiently for Have Heart to perform. The five-member band shared the stage with dozens of friends who wanted to be close to the action. Arguably more people were now on the stage than had been in the entire audience at their earliest shows. Seven years after forming, Have Heart had reached the top of their game and gained an international following, but just as Ten Yard Fight had done a decade earlier, they were ready to bow out after accomplishing everything they had ever dreamed of for their band.

The guitarist started strumming the opening notes of the song "Roland" by indie-rock band Interpol, with the drummer and bassist joining in and layering the sound. The crowd swayed back and forth in anticipation like ocean waves, packed together so tightly the movement wasn't entirely voluntary. An ambitious crowd surfer in a white T-shirt climbed up on top of fans and tried crawling across their heads to get closer to the stage. Dual stage divers with boogie boards ran from behind the band and leaped in unison onto the crowd as vocalist Pat Flynn, with a navy blue Red Sox hat perched atop his head, began to loudly shout the lyrics of their first song of the night, "Hard Bark on the Family Tree," into the microphone.

October leaves on Massachusetts' trees
A sight so fleetingly free
Just how October leaves
Just how October leaves
Just how October leaves
Me
On fire with the maple trees
On my knees with these leaves on these Boston streets
Praying to a god a godforsaken summer night stole
(One night), one fight, one family swallowed whole.

Everyone inside the Wonderland Ballroom sang along to every word, as each crowd surfer tumbled over the edge between the first row of fans onto the stage, and another person ran past the band and leaped off the monitors back into the audience. For each Have Heart fan in the crowd—even the ones in the back—that participation was part of the experience. But to someone who had never seen a hardcore band perform in their element like this, it looked like absolute chaos. A prison riot. A tragic accident waiting to happen.

Four minutes into the set, a Revere police officer working a detail inside of the club had seen enough. He walked onto the stage in his uniform and tried to stop the fans from jumping into the crowd. This caught the attention of Pat and the rest of the band, and the music abruptly stopped. Aware that situations and misunderstandings like this had gotten shows shut down midset in the past, Pat realized he needed to address the moment and how it was being perceived by someone not versed in punk: "What I think is the matter here," Pat spoke into the microphone, "is that to an outsider, this sometimes looks like people are trying to kill themselves. But I just want to clarify that we should let the outside world that is at this show tonight [know] that we're not here to kill each other. We're here for a good time, and we're looking out for each other. Is that right?"

That drew enthusiastic applause from the audience. Every fan knew the score: If someone fell to the ground, you picked them up. If someone knocked into you, it wasn't personal.

Pat continued, "We also want to have a good time. We've been doing this for seven years, and all we're asking is that you take care of each other, okay? Everyone here needs to get along. This [show] is a benefit for a women's shelter in New Bedford, Massachusetts. So if you happen to fall onstage, keep in mind there is an outside world here that may not understand this, so get rowdy, get fucking crazy, have a good time. Let's respect this place and respect each other!"

The police officer relented, and the band started their second song, "The Machinist." The rate of stage diving increased twofold, making it difficult to see what the band was doing with all the movement around them. Have Heart continued playing for more than an hour, and the crowd never let up, despite moving for most of the night in a room hotter than a midsummer afternoon in a New Orleans warehouse. Their final song, "Watch Me Rise," had the stage completely overrun with fans singing every word, the band completely hidden from view. As the final notes faded from the speakers, people began clapping and chanting the band's name, over and over again.

"Have Heart! Have Heart! Have Heart!"

It started slowly, from a group of people close to the stage. Each time it was repeated, it got louder, until many in the crowd had joined. As the moment passed and the people who had joined the band onstage to sing along began to hop down to the dance floor and disperse, Aaron—one of Bridge Nine's earliest employees and a longtime friend and supporter of Have Heart—stopped at the edge of the stage. He had sold shirts for me at Fenway for years and was the guy Tiger joked had been arrested when I was on the opposite coast in 2004. He was also the person who had lobbied hardest for me to listen to Have Heart's demo, ensuring I'd sign the band to the label and be a part of the magic that had unfolded tonight.

Aaron stood there with a huge grin, wearing a crisp white T-shirt. Like at the Ten Yard Fight show a decade earlier, friends made shirts to commemorate the event. Aaron sported one such tee with a familiar design. One inspired by ten seasons of hawking in-your-face T-shirts after Red Sox games and the innate desire to break your friend's balls, *especially* when they were on top of the world. The T-shirt stated: "Have Heart SUCKS." And it became an instant collector's item. With this chapter of the band officially over, things in the music scene would shift again. The baton would be passed to the new generation of punks, many of whom will be hawking Sully's Brand T-shirts for me outside of the next Bruins game. Then their bands would head into studios to record music for my record label. And all of it would be paid for by Boston sports fans.

AFTERWORD

A LOT HAS HAPPENED OVER THE MANY YEARS SINCE THE EVENTS I related in these pages happened. I'll try to sum it up here.

Galle went from putting local bands in VFW halls to national acts in arenas. He moved to New York City and, in 2006, helped launch the Photo Finish Records label, where he landed a gold record with the band 3OH!3. As an agent, he began working with a then unknown band called My Chemical Romance after first booking them from our Salem office in 2003. He later oversaw their 2022 reunion tour, which included two sold-out performances at the TD Garden, home of the Boston Celtics and Bruins. In 2025, he booked their *Long Live The Black Parade* tour and flew back to Boston with his family on a privately chartered jet for their sold-out performance at Fenway Park. Galle is, by all accounts, the most successful out of all of us, an acknowledgement that I am happy to report, but seriously never saw coming.

There must have been something magical about the Initech space, because each member's contributions to the music that excited them continued to evolve after it closed. Galle's partner at the Kenmore Booking Agency, Matt Pike, co-founded the 33 & West talent agency in Los Angeles and among many other, represents the bands Dance Gavin Dance, Cave In, and Converge, the latter two friends he first started booking shows for in the mid-1990s.

Jen Malone's company Black and White went from public relations to music supervision, and she's now an Emmy-nominated music supervisor with the shows *Euphoria* (HBO), *Atlanta* (FX), and *Mr. & Mrs. Smith* (Amazon) amongst her credits.

Rama's Big Wheel Recreation label went on hiatus sometime in 2004, but he's recently partnered with the Iodine Recordings label to re-issue some of his back catalog. Rama has also found success as an entrepreneur in the cannabis industry with his branding firm Green Street and Hall of Flowers trade show.

Aaron Turner's Hydra Head Records became inactive in 2020, but in addition to having performed with his bands ISIS, Sumac, Old Man Gloom, and countless others, Aaron continues to release music on his SIGE Records label, which he co-founded with his partner Faith Coloccia in 2014.

Max Powers moved to Los Angeles, where his constant hustle earned him a job as Snoop Dogg's assistant. The two costarred in the dark comedy film *Indiana Pill Runner*. Max later received a bachelor of arts degree from Berklee College of Music, majoring in songwriting and music production, and is now working on his master's degree.

Worm left Boston for New York City, where he became a fixture in the nightclub scene in the mid-2000s. These days he's living in North Carolina, is an avid horse-racing gambler, and roots for the Mets.

Rod returned to his hometown in upstate New York, and we kept in touch for a while, usually around the holidays. On social media, he still refers to himself as an "International Man of Leisure."

Jesse Standhard got his real-estate license and has been crushing sales records while selling homes for the past decade, including helping me land the condo I live in now. He and his wife, Val, are raising their daughter in Greater Boston.

Wes Eisold, ever the creative, went on to front several new musical projects after American Nightmare, including the hardcore-punk band Some Girls and the darkwave, synthpop band Cold Cave, which has shared the stage with bands like Soundgarden, Nine Inch Nails, and Depeche Mode. American Nightmare reunited in 2011, seven years after they'd initially called it quits, and continues to tour and release new music. Wes lives in Los Angeles, is married, has a young son, and owns Heartworm Press, a book-publishing and record-label imprint.

The Bouncer moved to Los Angeles as an aspiring filmmaker. However, after publicly leaving his gang life behind, he was arrested for an unrelated extortion case from events that had transpired years earlier. Despite a supportive group of A-list actors who recognized his talent having written letters to the court on his behalf, he ended up doing a year in federal prison. Still, he persevered and, once released, returned to LA and has found success as a writer, director, and producer.

After thirty-six years of service as a Codee for the City of Boston, Tiger can technically retire whenever he's ready. However, he recently told me he has another fifteen years left in him. I was invited to Tiger's wedding as a guest twenty-two years after he first chased me around Fenway Park, and I count him as a close friend.

Elisabeth and I married in the summer of 2005. She supported my ideas and my work, and I would not have made it this far without her in my corner. In 2011 our daughter, Georgia, was born. Elisabeth and I later divorced, finding we were better suited as friends, and now successfully coparent in our modern family with our respective new partners.

I'm still at it with Bridge Nine and Sully's. In 2004 I signed a distribution deal with Universal Music, and in the years since, influential, genre-defining artists like Defeater, Gallows, War on Women, Polar Bear Club, Frank Turner, and Dropkick Murphys have also released music on Bridge Nine. Thirty years after that first 7-inch single, the label has released more than three hundred recordings with a catalog that has gone on to include some of the world's biggest and best hardcore-punk bands.

Out of the same warehouse, Sully's continues to design and distribute the favorite T-shirts of Boston fans worldwide, now catering to the grown children of our earliest customers. I later bought out the stake Jesse Standhard had inherited from Worm, absorbing the Suckers' operation into Sully's. Hawking shirts on the sidewalk remained a right of passage for Boston's hardcore punks for seventeen years, making the most of every championship push and celebratory parade.

When an account of our crew of "Yankees Suck" vendors was first published in 2015 by the ESPN-backed *Grantland* sports and pop culture blog, and then again in 2017 by ESPN's *30 for 30* podcast, I learned that almost all references to my involvement had been omitted, despite having been interviewed extensively for both pieces. I was annoyed at first, but their focus was squarely on the party culture and drug use by the Suckers, a narrative I wanted nothing to do with. A photograph of the "Yankees Suck" crew featuring me front and center included in the article almost derailed a sponsorship with the Jimmy Fund charity that I was negotiating for Sully's the same week the *Grantland* story came out. Thankfully, I was given the benefit of the doubt, and my collaboration with the Jimmy Fund was a success.

The Sully's brand is now distributed in Target stores, including a location next to Fenway Park. It's across the street from where the old Initech office once stood before it was torn down to make way for a fourteen-story building with a swimming pool on the roof. The "Believe in Boston" slogan I trademarked back in 2004 has raised more than $150,000 for local charities, and the sales of those T-shirts significantly outpaced "Yankees Suck" tees years ago. After the Red Sox won the 2018 World Series in Los Angeles, most of the team partied on the plane ride home with the Commissioner's Trophy while wearing "Believe in Boston" sweatshirts. Months after I met Boston mayor Marty Walsh at a charity event and gave him a "Believe in Boston" shirt, he made it the theme of his 2020 State of the City address. In 2023 we landed a licensing deal for the slogan with Dunkin' Brands after Ben Affleck was regularly photographed wearing our "Believe in Boston" T-shirts while carrying their coffee. And when the Celtics won the NBA Finals in 2024, almost every Duck Boat in their parade had someone waving one of our flags. "Believe in Boston" has become the mantra of every sports team in the city. I couldn't be prouder of that.

In June 2020, during the first months of the COVID-19 pandemic, I was told by our longtime landlord that the building that housed Bridge Nine and Sully's was being sold. The rent would double if we wanted to remain a tenant under the new owner. I took a risk, sold everything I could (including my Liberated Images screen-printing business), and bought a run-down 1930s-era car dealer building two towns over in February 2021. The day after I closed on the property, a location scout for the film *The Tender Bar* called, inquiring if they could rent and redecorate it as a '70s-era Photo Hut film-developing studio. As it turned out, the "Dickens Bar" where they would be filming the exterior shots was one storefront over. The movie was directed by George Clooney and starred Affleck, and the fee that they paid helped cover the first month of our mortgage. I saw it as a sign from the universe that I was moving in the right direction, as Ben Affleck had been a longtime supporter of Sully's and had worn our T-shirts for years. He had even famously worn one of our "Believe in Boston" tees in his film *The Town*.

They say to buy the worst house on the best block, right? Overwhelmed by the undertaking, I then spent the next eighteen months renovating and upgrading the run-down space, with help from a rotating cast of friends and supporters—most prominently, Larry Kelley, who contributed several hundred afternoons volunteering his time, tools, and expertise. After all that work, the result is a beautiful retail, warehouse, and performance space that Bridge Nine and Sully's Brand share at 282 Rantoul Street in Beverly, one town over from the Witch City of Salem and about thirty-five minutes north of Boston, the city where it all began. In addition to offering a curated selection of hardcore and punk vinyl and Sully's Brand T-shirts, we've also hosted intimate live performances by some of our favorite artists: New Found Glory, American Nightmare, Cave In, H2O, and Agnostic Front. We even had Ten Yard Fight last fall for their first official Greater Boston area show since their swan song in 1999, when they decided to do a small warm-up gig with a live audience before heading to Birmingham, Alabama, to play in front of a much bigger crowd at the annual Furnace Festival.

When my daughter, Georgia, was six years old, I helped her start her own brand, Georgia Made This, to feature her whimsical illustrations. Sully's had been selling T-shirts to tourists visiting Salem during October's Halloween season, and Georgia asked if she could make a T-shirt too. I took her drawings of a ghost, pumpkin, and a skull and printed a box of Salem T-shirts, which she sold from her modified lemonade stand on the sidewalk. They were gone over a weekend, and within two seasons, her brand was outselling mine. By year three, I stopped bringing Sully's products to Salem and focused on her efforts. I started a 529 college savings plan with the proceeds, and we've put enough away for her first two years. Her artwork proved so popular that in 2025 we moved her booth into a year-round brick-and-mortar store called Georgia's Little Salem Shop, inside the nineteenth-century building where her first monsters were drawn at the coffeehouse next door. At thirteen she became the Witch City's youngest shopkeeper, and a new family tradition of starting a brand on a sidewalk continued into a second generation. And to think at her age, I was making just three dollars an hour raking leaves.

In 2023 I married the love of my life, Katherine. With her by my side I feel like anything is possible. Tiger attended our wedding and continues to be one of my biggest supporters. Katherine and I live and work together running our collection of brands in Beverly, Massachusetts. In 2025, we welcomed the birth of our daughter (and Georgia's highly anticipated little sister), Eleanor Mae.

Yankee hating had fallen out of fashion as the Red Sox collected three more World Series titles in 2007, 2013, and 2018, while the Yankees earned just one in 2009. We kept some of our rivalry gear in stock but retired most of it, continuing to focus our energy on what makes Boston great, instead of punching down. We did, however, have some fun in 2018 when Red Sox pitcher Joe Kelly reignited the rivalry after hitting Yankees utility player Tyler Austin with a pitch. The purposeful beaning was in response to Tyler having slid into Red Sox shortstop Brock Holt with his cleats dangerously high earlier in the game, a maneuver known as "spiking," in an attempt to derail a double play. We printed "Joe Kelly Fight Club" T-shirts the next morning to commemorate the bench-clearing brawl that ensued, and it became one of our bestsellers that season, helping Joe raise money for his anti-human trafficking charity, a silver lining to the six-game suspension he was handed down by Major League Baseball. A popular 2020 reprint of the shirt after Joe started pitching for the Los Angeles Dodgers helped us keep the lights on during the pandemic, when most of our other business efforts were in limbo. Thank you for that, Joe and Ashley Kelly!

Disdain for the Yankees clearly remains almost fifty years after Joe Schatzle Jr. sold the first "Yankees Suck" T-shirt outside of Fenway Park and twenty-six years after my friends and I first started hawking "Yankees Suck" merchandise, so a third generation has filled the void that we left behind. The popular slogan has become available once again after Red Sox games from two brothers, Mohammed and Riad. First nicknamed the "Candy Boys" from their time spent selling candy bars on Lansdowne Street as children, they grew up as street vendors outside of Fenway Park. Now known as "the Fenway Brothers," they promote their own line of Sully's-influenced shirts from a newspaper kiosk that they rent from the city on the section of sidewalk in Kenmore Square where I made most of my sales. And when the Yankees come to town our friend Sly, who owns the independent magazine *The Yawkey Way Report*, still includes a "Yankees Suck" sticker with each copy sold.

Three decades after releasing my first vinyl record, I still feel like I'm making things up as I go, and I occasionally struggle with feelings of imposter syndrome. But the list of cool shit I've done and have helped others to do has grown pretty long, so I know I'm doing something right. When I started the Bridge Nine label, I wanted to make a mark and be a part of something bigger than myself. Despite not truly knowing what I was doing, I pulled together whatever resources I could, releasing those first few singles to contribute to a subculture that had become so important to me. But taking it from the local band level to an internationally recognized brand required an investment I didn't have and didn't think was accessible, one that didn't end up coming from a bank or a wealthy investor but came from what I earned on the sidewalks and streets around Fenway Park. I found a way to take hundreds of thousands of dollars from baseball fans and pumped that money into a generation of hardcore-punk bands so they could be heard around the world. The resulting journey completely changed the game for the bands I love and continues to open more doors for me than I ever would have imagined.

ACKNOWLEDGMENTS

AS SOMEONE WHO HAS EMBRACED THE "DO IT YOURSELF" ethos, I've learned that while I may start things on my own, I'll need a lot of help along the way to see them through. I want to thank my wife, Katherine, for her unwavering love and support during the many years that it took to write this book. From helping talk through ideas, reading early drafts, and offering my first feedback, your assistance and encouragement helped give me the confidence to see this through.

I want to thank Randall Lotowycz, my editor at Running Press/Hachette Book Group, for his thoughtful advice and support. This book is better because of your guidance. Thank you to Amber Morris, my production editor at HBG, for making the editorial production process so smooth. I also want to thank my literary agent, Joseph Perry, for taking a chance on my manuscript and for your suggestions on how to improve it. And most important, for helping this first-time author land a publishing deal with the best partner possible.

I want to thank one of my most loyal friends, Larry Kelley, for reading my early drafts and offering me feedback, but also for always checking in and helping keep the other stuff around me moving while I was so focused on finishing this.

Thank you to my friends and family who also took the time to speak with me about the events that transpired in this book, offered encouragement, and provided actionable feedback, including Elisabeth Wrenn, Wesley Eisold, Max Powers, Ray Hogan, Benjamin Gibson, Ian McFarland, Matt Breen, Gibby Miller, Mike Gitter, Derek Archambault, Christopher Stockbridge, Duane Lucia, and Jared Carrabis.

Thank you to Irene Dondley and Joe Schatzle Jr. for speaking with me about your experiences peddling T-shirts in the same streets around Fenway Park in the 1970s.

I would also like to thank author Nancy Barile for being an early reader and vocal supporter and for introducing me to Raquel Pidal, who had edited her book *I'm Not Holding Your Coat: My Bruises-and-All Memoir of Punk Rock Rebellion*. Raquel, thank you for your extensive editing feedback on how to best structure this story and for making the introduction to my literary agent!

I would like to thank Sarah Herritage, Meg Price, Jess Humphrey, Kate Bowen, Hugo Fitz, Bryan Sheffield, Kevin P. Coughlin, Matt Stone, Jeff Lasich, Todd Pollock, and Derek Kouyoumjian for documenting these moments and for allowing me to use their photographs to help illustrate this story.

And thank you to Dave Wedge, author of *Boston Strong* and *Hunting Whitey*. Dave and I had never met, but we shared mutual connections in the Boston sports and music world, so I sent him a message after I finished my first draft, hoping to speak with someone who'd done it all as an author. Dave obliged. Thank you for taking the time to meet and for your insight and advice.

ABOUT THE AUTHOR

SINCE HIS SALAD DAYS AS A TEENAGE SKATEBOARDER, CHRIS Wrenn has focused on two tasks: documenting the music of his favorite bands and finding unusual ways to pay for it. The indie record label that he started three decades ago in his college dorm room, Bridge Nine, has gained an international following by releasing more than three hundred recordings from some of the most impactful bands in the punk-music underground. At the same time, Sully's, the Beantown-centric brand that Chris founded with an initial goal—to earn the money needed to fund the record label—went from profiting on bitter sports rivalries to celebrating all things Boston. The slogan that he coined in the spring of 2004, "Believe in Boston," has become a rallying cry embraced by all of the city's professional sports teams twenty years later.

Chris and his wife, Katherine, live and work thirty-five minutes north of Boston (and one town over from the Witch City of Salem) in Beverly, Massachusetts. Together they are raising a toddler and a teenager while also managing the day-to-day responsibilities of both brands. You can visit the dual Bridge Nine and Sully's retail store at 282 Rantoul Street in Beverly and learn more about what Chris is up to next at www.ChrisWrenn.com.

RAISING READERS

Books Build Bright Futures

Thank you for reading this book and for being a reader of books in general. As
author, I am so grateful to share being part of a community of readers with yo
and I hope you will join me in passing our love of books on to the next generati
of readers.

Did you know that reading for enjoyment is the single biggest predictor of child's future happiness and success?

More than family circumstances, parents' educational background, or incom reading impacts a child's future academic performance, emotional well-bein communication skills, economic security, ambition, and happiness.

Studies show that kids reading for enjoyment in the US is in rapid decline:

- In 2012, 53% of 9-year-olds read almost every day. Just 10 years later, in 2022, the number had fallen to 39%.
- In 2012, 27% of 13-year-olds read for fun daily. By 2023, that number was just 14%.

Together, we can commit to **Raising Readers** and change this trend. How?

- Read to children in your life daily.
- Model reading as a fun activity.
- Reduce screen time.
- Start a family, school, or community book club.
- Visit bookstores and libraries regularly.
- Listen to audiobooks.
- Read the book before you see the movie.
- Encourage your child to read aloud to a pet or stuffed animal.
- Give books as gifts.
- Donate books to families and communities in need.

BOB1217

Books build bright futures, and **Raising Readers** is our shared responsibility.

For more information, visit **JoinRaisingReaders.com**

Sources: National Endowment for the Arts, National Assessment of Educational Progress, WorldBookDay.org, Nielsen BookData's 2023 "Understanding the Children's Book Consumer"